MW00985618

Mighty, Mighty
MATADORS

Swaim-Paup-Foran Spirit of Sport Series

Sponsored by James C. '74 and Debra Parchman Swaim, Nancy and T. Edgar Paup '74, and Joseph Wm. and Nancy Foran

Mighty, Mighty
MATADORS

∞

Estacado High School, Integration,
and a Championship Season

Al Pickett

TEXAS A&M UNIVERSITY PRESS
COLLEGE STATION

This paper meets the requirements of ANSI/NISO Z39.48–1992
(Permanence of Paper).
Binding materials have been chosen for durability.
Manufactured in the United States of America

LIBRARY OF CONGRESS CATALOGING-IN-PUBLICATION DATA
Names: Pickett, Al, author.
Title: Mighty, mighty Matadors : Estacado High School, integration, and a
    championship season / Al Pickett.
Other titles: Swaim-Paup-Foran spirit of sport series.
Description: First edition. | College Station : Texas A&M University Press,
    [2017] | Series: Swaim-Paup-Foran spirit of sport series | Includes index.
Identifiers: LCCN 2016059089 (print) | LCCN 2017006055 (ebook) | ISBN
    9781623495510 (cloth : alk. paper) | ISBN 9781623495527 (ebook)
Subjects: LCSH: Estacado Matadors (Football team)—History—20th century. |
    Estacado Matadors (Football team)—Biography. | Estacado High School
    (Lubbock, Tex.)—Football—History—20th century. | School
    integration—Texas—Lubbock—History—20th century.
Classification: LCC GV959.53.L83 P53 2017 (print) | LCC GV959.53.L83
    (ebook) | DDC 796.332/6209764847—dc23
LC record available at https://lccn.loc.gov/2016059089

*This book is dedicated to Coach Jimmie Keeling
and the 1968 Lubbock Estacado Matadors,
who were such a tremendous help in allowing me to tell the
remarkable story of their state championship season.*

Contents

Galleries of images follow pages 45 and 70.

Mighty, Mighty
MATADORS

Introduction

Who Are the Matadors?
We Are the Matadors!
The Mighty, Mighty Matadors!
Weeeeeeee are the Matadors,
Fiiiiiighting Matadors.
Stop Look and Listen
Here Come the Mighty Matadors
Stop Look and Listen
Here Come the Mighty Matadors
(Repeat)
Stop!

J immie Keeling says he still gets chills when he thinks about that chant. "On the days we had a pep rally before our game, the team would meet in the dressing room and then march together to the auditorium for the pep rally," recalled Keeling, who was a young thirty-one-year-old head coach when he accepted the job to start the football program at Estacado, Lubbock Independent School District's newest high school, in 1967 in Lubbock, Texas. "The minute the team stepped out of the dressing room, they started chanting, 'We are the Matadors, the Mighty, Mighty Matadors.' As classes let out for the pep rally, the other students joined in. Pretty soon, 'We are the Matadors, the Mighty Matadors' would be ringing through the whole school."

The layout of the new school situated all competitive athletics dressing rooms in the southwest corner of the school complex. Entry to this dedicated area was through a set of double doors, just beyond the school's gymnasium and across from its cafeteria. Through these doors, athletes entered a long hallway, and along this corridor were the individual doorways into the dressing rooms of each competitive sport—tennis, track, baseball, basketball, and football. Varsity football was about halfway down this hallway. The players, chanting in unison, exited the dressing room and advanced two or three abreast up the corridor to the double doors that opened into the main classroom complex. As soon as they began to pass through these doors en route to the auditorium the other students could hear them.

The chant would last until all of the students were inside the auditorium, the team had been seated up front, a cheerleader gave the signal, and the chant would end with a shout on the next "Stop."

Keeling was tasked with the assignment of building a football team from scratch at Estacado High School. But this wasn't any ordinary job. It was the first time the Lubbock Independent School District had a truly integrated school. Lubbock High had a handful of black students in 1966 and 1967, but Monterey and Coronado remained all white. Dunbar, the city's black high school, remained open as an all-black school. But Estacado was built and boundary lines were redrawn to take some white students from the Lubbock High attendance area and some black students from Dunbar to attend Estacado.

It had been a decade since President Dwight Eisenhower ordered federal troops to Little Rock, Arkansas, to allow seven black students to enter all-white Little Rock Central High School. In 1964, the Civil Rights Act ordered an end to segregation, forcing school districts to finally integrate the public schools. Interracial marriages were still illegal in Texas until 1967.

"It was an era of separate but not equal," David Moody, one of the black leaders of the Estacado football team who later returned to his alma mater as the head football coach, matter-of-factly stated.

Just months earlier, in March 1966, Texas Western University won the NCAA Midwest Regional basketball tournament in a double-overtime thriller over Kansas at the Lubbock Municipal Coliseum. The next week, the Miners made history when coach Don Haskins started five blacks and defeated an all-white Kentucky team to claim the NCAA title. That was the first time that a team playing five blacks had won the national basketball championship.

Change was coming slowly to the South and to Texas, however. By 1967 or 1968, most cities had closed their all-black schools and integrated them into their white schools.

Even in 1967 and 1968, Keeling said he had to select places to eat carefully because "some people wouldn't serve us pregame and postgame meals. They said the black players would have to eat in the kitchen. That was not that long ago."

A year after Estacado opened, the US Department of Health, Education, and Welfare claimed the Lubbock system was segregated and urged federal aid be cut. A hearing in June 1970 determined the system was in compliance and rejected the claim. Just two months later, however, the Justice Department filed suit against twenty-six Texas school districts, including Lubbock, charging them with operating segregated school systems.

According to the *Lubbock Avalanche-Journal*, the case landed in the courtroom of US District Judge Halbert O. Woodward, who would monitor the district's progress and hold the Lubbock Independent School District (LISD) accountable for the next twenty-one years. The suit eventually led to the busing of nearly 2,000 students daily and sowed the seeds for the development of magnet schools in the Lubbock school district.

In the fall of 1967, however, Lubbock's integration plan involved just one high school, Estacado, and Keeling's Matadors became so much more than just a football team. The team became the rallying focal point for northeast Lubbock, proof that black, brown, and white students could not only go to school together

but could also bond together as a successful football team to become a unifying force for the entire school.

That was evident some forty-five years later when Keeling
and seven members of his team gathered at teammate Tommy
Scruggs's farm home just outside Lubbock to meet with me to
first kick off the idea of writing a book about their state championship season of 1968.

As I met with the former players—white, black, and Hispanic—
I was struck with the obvious, genuine friendship that existed.
It was not that they wanted to brag about their remarkable un-
defeated season. Instead, it was recognition that they had been
a part of something special nearly a half century earlier; it was a
story they wanted to share.

They had not remained close friends because they won a state
championship together. They were close friends because they had
experienced the same ups and downs, the same hard work and
dedication, and the same successes and failures together. In a time
when the world had seemingly gone a little crazy and everything
they thought they knew had been turned upside down, this group
of mostly sixteen- and seventeen-year-old boys had put team
ahead of self and took an entire school and city on a magical ride.

And later, in 1968 after this team had won ten games in remarkable fashion to secure a district title and a playoff berth,
they would become a point of pride for an entire city. Politicians,
prominent citizens, businesses, and students representing the
other four high schools in the LISD would attend the Matadors'
pep rallies and voice their support for the team's state championship dream. Everyone, it seemed, wanted to go along on this
magical ride.

Remember, this was the era of the Vietnam War and protests to the war, the hippie movement and psychedelic music,
integration, race riots, and the assassinations of Martin Luther
King and Robert Kennedy. It was with that backdrop that Keel-

ing and his Matadors forged a common goal—to be the best football team they could be. What they accomplished was truly remarkable.

"The story about this team is historic," emphasized Pete Ragus, the octogenarian who spent twenty-four years as the athletic director for the LISD. He is the one who hired Keeling for the job and put many of the pieces in place for Estacado to be successful. "The 1968 Estacado team is the only team in LISD history to win a University Interscholastic League [UIL] state football championship since Lubbock became a multi-UIL school system in 1955 with the addition of Monterey High School. Since 1955, no other football team in LISD has won a UIL state championship. This team was also the only team in UIL history, to my knowledge, to win a state football championship during its first year in varsity competition. So many interesting stories about this team are historic."

Actually, Estacado is one of just two high schools in Texas high school football history to win a state championship in its first season of varsity football. But it was the first, and it was the only "new" school to do it. Fourteen years after Estacado claimed a state championship, Beaumont West Brook captured a Class 5A state title in 1982 in its first season as a football program. But West Brook was actually a consolidated school between shuttered Forest Park and Hebert High Schools in Beaumont, and the Bruins stumbled into the playoffs as a district runner-up with a lackluster 5–4–1 record before catching fire and winning a state title.

The championship season at Beaumont West Brook can't compare to what Estacado accomplished—both on and off the field—in 1968.

Now, so many years later, we think nothing of athletic teams and schools with mixed races competing together. It is commonplace. But it wasn't always that way. Someone or some team had to be the first to prove that color didn't matter. Someone or some team had to prove that it would work. In Lubbock, that team was the Estacado Matadors.

Linebacker David Moody said the Matadors were the real story, the "Remember the Titans," before the Titans.

This is the story of the 1968 Estacado football team, the Mighty, Mighty Matadors who overcame all odds to be state champions.

Chapter 1

Square Dance to State Champ

J ust as Jimmie Keeling was getting out of the car, Nat Williams asked him, "You do realize you are the most important person for this to be successful?"

Keeling had just accepted the head football coaching job at Estacado High School, a new school that hadn't even opened yet, in Lubbock, Texas. Years later, Keeling recalled his hiring at Estacado as the most unusual in his hall of fame career that spanned more than fifty years.

Olan Rice, who was going to be the principal of the new high school, was sitting in the car in the parking lot of the Lubbock Independent School District administration building on that cold early January day along with Keeling, LISD athletic director Pete Ragus, LISD personnel director Robert Knight, and Williams, the school district's longtime superintendent.

"Well, I know my job is important," Keeling responded, admittedly stammering a bit in his uncertainty of how to answer the question, especially with Rice, the school's new principal, in the car, too.

"No, you are the most important person for this to be successful," emphasized Williams, repeating himself.

Lubbock Independent School District was opening a new high school in the fall of 1967, the third new high school to be built in the growing Hub City on the South Plains in the last twelve years. But Estacado would be vastly different from Monterey and Coronado, both all-white high schools that had opened since 1955. Until the addition of Monterey and Coronado, Lubbock, like most cities across Texas, had been a two-high-school town— all-white Lubbock High and all-black Dunbar High, which had historically participated in the Texas Prairie View Interscholastic League (first named the Texas Interscholastic League of Colored Schools), not the University Interscholastic League (UIL) with the city's other high schools. The races had not mixed in the city's public school system until the last year or two when just a handful of black students enrolled at Lubbock High or Alderson Junior High.

In fact, the UIL implemented full integration of all governed academic, music, arts, and athletic competitions for the first time in the fall of 1967. From the 1920s through 1966, the Prairie View Interscholastic League (PVIL) had played the leading role in creating and overseeing competitive activities for all-black schools in Texas. The PVIL staged playoffs and championships in football, basketball, baseball, and track and field. At its peak, the PVIL included five hundred all-black schools across Texas.

Lubbock Dunbar had a proud tradition in PVIL athletics, especially in basketball. Dunbar won five PVIL state basketball championships between 1953 and 1965 ('53, '57, '60, '62, and '65) to very little fanfare.

Unlike in most other West Texas cities, however, the Lubbock school board had decided not to close its all-black school in 1967. Dunbar, instead, would remain open, but Estacado would serve the northeast side of Lubbock, taking students from Alderson Junior High, the feeder school for Lubbock High, and Struggs Junior High, the feeder for Dunbar, as well as a handful of students from Lubbock High School and Dunbar in the newly redrawn district boundaries.

Why did the LISD board of trustees keep Dunbar open rather than closing it when Estacado opened? "The only people who know the answer to that are the seven school board members," Ragus responded nearly fifty years later. "We do not understand that ourselves. We have never found out. There is conjecture, but the facts we don't know. But this is what happened. When everyone else was closing their black schools—Midland, Odessa, Wichita Falls, and Abilene—the school board voted one week 4–3 to close Dunbar. About a week later, the school board met again and voted 4–3 to keep Dunbar open the way it is. Now what happened during that week, nobody knows." Ragus continued:

> But the facts of that were true. But why it happened, you would almost have to go the school board members and find out. But it changed the entire dynamic situation in regard to our competitive situation in Lubbock. If that school had been closed like Midland, Odessa, and the other towns, it would have put Monterey and Coronado into a totally different circumstance in the use of athletes you need to win ball games. It would have helped integration, too, which was the purpose of the whole thing, not to have a better football team, but to integrate. We didn't do that. We ended up with two black schools.
>
> We didn't close Dunbar until 1993 or '94. All those years from 1967 to the early 1990s, we were operating in a total different circumstance than the other schools we were competing against. We ended up with less integration and two black schools instead of one.

Although the school district officials simply talked about opening a new school, not making an issue of the historical significance of Estacado, everyone realized that it would be the city's first truly integrated high school. Williams and the LISD administration were carefully handpicking the staff and faculty that would be in place when Estacado opened in the fall, and Williams understood the role that football could play in unifying the new school and making the city's first attempt at integration a success.

"I worked with a lot of great people at Estacado," Keeling stated. "Everyone who was at Estacado wanted to be there."

Not even the venerable superintendent, however, could have foreseen just how accurate his statement was to Keeling on that early January day in 1967.

When coaches interview for new jobs, they usually meet with several committees, according to Keeling, and then come back for a final interview with the school board. He said his hiring for the Estacado job was much simpler, however.

Keeling took his first head coaching job at Dublin in West Texas in 1959 and then moved to Tulia in the Texas Panhandle in 1961, where he spent the next five seasons. During his stint at Tulia, Keeling interviewed for the coaching job at Lubbock Coronado. "I was a finalist for the Coronado job," Keeling recalled, "although they hired Wayne Wilscher. But through that process of interviewing for the Coronado job, I developed a good relationship with Pete Ragus."

In 1966, Keeling moved to Elgin in Central Texas. Keeling said he enjoyed his year at Elgin, which gave him the opportunity to attend Darrell Royal's two-a-day workouts at the nearby University of Texas. "We had a reasonable year," Keeling said of Elgin. "They were going to be good the next year."

Elgin Washington, the city's all-black high school, was closing after the 1966–67 school year and merging with Elgin High School. Keeling often attended Washington's games, which were usually played on Thursday nights, to get to know the new players who would be on his team the next year.

During the middle of the 1966 season, however, Keeling said he received a letter in the mail from Ragus, describing Estacado, the new integrated high school that Lubbock was opening the next fall.

"Would you be interested?" Ragus asked in the letter.

Keeling, who said he was busy with the Elgin football season, recalled he took Ragus's letter and wrote on it, "Definitely, yes."

He mailed it back to Ragus and didn't think about it again—until the Christmas holidays.

School was still out of session for the holidays when Keeling went up to his office one morning. A custodian was there, cleaning in preparation for the start of the second semester the following week. "Hi, Coach," the custodian greeted Keeling. "Your phone rang, so I answered it. I left a message under your phone."

The call was from Ragus, asking Keeling to call him.

"We would like to talk to you about the Estacado job," said Ragus when Keeling returned his call. "Could you be here in the morning?"

So Keeling took off for the seven-hour drive to Lubbock, spending the night with a friend there. The next morning, he met Ragus, Williams, Rice, and Knight at the administration building at 7:00 a.m. "We got in the car and went to a restaurant for breakfast," he recalled. "We talked for a long time, and then we drove out to Estacado. It was a just the hull of a building. We went all over the high school and kept talking and talking. By that time, it was time for lunch, so we drove back to the same restaurant for lunch."

Following lunch, the group drove back to the Lubbock Independent School District administration building.

"Would you mind waiting outside?" Williams asked Keeling, who stepped outside while the other four men discussed his hiring.

"It was freezing cold," Keeling said. "It seemed like I was standing outside forever, but it was probably only about ten minutes when Mr. Williams motioned me to get back in the car."

"Can you be here Monday?" Williams asked.

"Yes, sir," Keeling replied, "but I've got to go back to Elgin and get released from my contract."

And just like that—after breakfast, lunch, and a meeting in a car in the parking lot—Keeling was headed to Lubbock to become the first head football coach at Estacado High School.

"We were in a big, big search for a coach," Ragus remembered. "We interviewed a number of coaches and had a lot of people apply. But the bottom line is Jimmie impressed me and our committee more than any other person. He had a nice record. He had a nice way with kids. He had everything we were looking for. Estacado was a unique circumstance, a black school with a few Hispanics and a few Anglos. We were looking for a unique person who would work in that situation. With all the people we talked to, we came up with the fact that he was the right person who could work in this circumstance. We couldn't have been more right."

Ragus knew all about the important role that a football team could play in integration. Just seven years earlier, he was the head coach at Corpus Christi Miller in 1960 when he led the Buccaneers team, which had eighteen whites, seventeen Hispanics, and six blacks, including future NFL star Johnny Roland, on its roster, to a state championship. Miller was the first Texas team to win a UIL state championship with three different ethnic groups. Ragus compiled a 57–13–1 record at Miller, including a 13–1 mark in 1960 that resulted in a state championship. He was named the Texas High School Coach of the Year in 1960.

When school in Lubbock resumed on the following Monday, Keeling was assigned to Lubbock High where he spent the mornings during the spring semester coteaching square dancing in a coed physical education class.

"Actually, I had," Keeling responded when asked if he had ever done any square dancing before. "I tell people my career went from square dancing to state champ."

After spending the mornings at Lubbock High, Keeling went to Alderson Junior High where he spent the afternoons. During sixth period, the football players who planned to play football next fall at Estacado were bused to Alderson for off-season workouts. The players came from Struggs, and there were also a few from Lubbock High and Dunbar who joined the players from Alderson.

Keeling said he had nine sophomores for those first off-season workouts. The rest were all ninth graders.

During that first week of the second semester, all of the students who would be enrolled in Estacado the next fall attended an assembly at the Alderson Junior High auditorium. Williams, Ragus, and Rice were there to explain the plans for the new school. Keeling, however, was the guest speaker. "I remember I talked about Philippians, that all things were possible through Christ," Keeling said.

Years later, David Moody, who became one of the Matadors' defensive leaders and later followed Keeling into the coaching ranks, admitted that he and his friends thought that the little short guy (Keeling) sitting on the stage with the superintendent and principal at the assembly that day was the truant officer.

Little did they know that the "truant officer" would change their lives forever.

Chapter 2

Putting the Pieces Together

J immie Keeling faced a daunting task as he met his future
players for the first time during the sixth period at Alderson
Junior High. Not only did he have to work at getting players
into shape, but he also had to determine who could play what position and to develop camaraderie among players of different races
and from different schools, many of whom didn't know each other.

"Very quickly, I realized that we had fast guys, a lot of talent,"
Keeling recalled. He continued:

> One of the real jobs was to not only take our best-skilled play-
> ers and make them running backs and defensive backs, but
> to take other guys who could have been backs and put them
> in the offensive and defensive lines. We had sprinters on the
> offensive line. They weren't typical linemen.
>
> It took some convincing at times. We communicated with
> them that we wanted to be the best we can be, and you might not
> play where you thought you would. There may have been some
> hurt feelings, but in time they all bought in. We saw some great-
> ness in them that initially they didn't see. We worked their tails
> off. We worked hard from Day One to be the best they can be.

Keeling said he had probably two dozen running backs, many of
whom needed to be moved to different positions. For example,
Robert Hines was moved to the offensive line. "He was a run-

ning back at Struggs when he got to us," Keeling said. "He was a sprinter. We convinced him to become an offensive lineman. He was a great one. He was a quiet guy, but when he did say something, the guys listened. He played extremely well."

Hines said he learned discipline as a member of the Matadors football team. "We learned that the coaches wouldn't let us do anything to disrespect the team or the school," he claimed.

Keeling put Frank Judie at fullback. "He was short but powerful," Keeling said. "He was a good runner, but he was such a great blocker. With Frank, we had a fullback who had great speed and could also run. He was a talented guy with a great spirit. Another asset was his physical toughness. He had fun, and he wanted to be good."

"The summer before Estacado opened, I weighed 145 pounds," Judie recalled. "I gained 25 pounds that summer. Maybe the coaches thought it was from working out, but the truth was that I had worked that summer at a burger joint, and I loved French fries and ketchup. I ate my way to 175 pounds. It turned out to be a better weight for me in football."

Keeling said David Moody was a team leader at linebacker. "He was so committed," he said of Moody. "He could do a lot of things. He played linebacker, but we could have put him in a hundred different places. He played some tight end. Our defense was unbelievable. We had great speed, but they bought in. David had great values, and he really helped us to be good because it was so important to him."

Keeling put James Lester in the secondary, where "he became a superior defensive back," and moved Bobby Lester to offensive guard. Keeling kept James Mosley and Larry Miller at running back, describing both as big running backs with good speed. James Lethridge was a little 140-pound running back, but Keeling said he could fly and was a change of pace to Mosley and Miller. Marvin Turner, the team's other fullback, became a great defensive back, according to Keeling.

"I couldn't have been more blessed with kids who could do a number of things," he said. "They were not necessarily typical for the position they were playing, but they had great speed. One of the most important things in coaching is putting guys in spots where they can be successful to help the team. It might not be where they had played before."

Kenneth Wallace was another running back who was moved to another position. "I went to their first (ninth grade) basketball game in January, and he scored an unbelievable number of points," Keeling continued. "He stood out. He had unbelievable quickness and skills. We started talking to him about how we wanted him to be our quarterback."

Wallace went on to play football at Texas Tech and for the Miami Dolphins. But in 1967, he was just trying to figure out how he fit into this new environment. Actually, Wallace, who is now an assistant superintendent in the Galena Park Independent School District in suburban Houston, experienced his first adjustment several months earlier on the first day of school.

He had enrolled the previous fall at Alderson Junior High, one of only a handful of African American students in the previously all-white school. "We had been living in an apartment [in the Dunbar district]," Wallace pointed out. "The summer before my ninth-grade year, my parents bought their first house, across the street from Alderson. The first day of school, my mom and dad had gone to work, so I caught a bus and went to Dunbar instead of going to Alderson like I was supposed to. The next morning, my mom escorted me to Alderson."

Wallace admitted that once football season started, he had no problems because his life was all about football. "I had played football in ninth grade, so people knew me," he stated. "I never faced any of the negative things that others might have. When Coach Keeling got here and we started spring practice, he put me at quarterback. I was the quarterback at the end of spring. Coach worked our butts off. It was like a camp. He corralled us and got in our minds. He started talking about winning. We lifted weights and did off-season competitive drills. After that spring, some people made up their minds that football was not really for them. It wasn't for the faint of heart."

Wallace, the youngest of three boys, said he had always been competitive, no matter what sport he was playing. But he was shocked when Coach Keeling put him at quarterback. "Coach Keeling had a confidence in me that I didn't see in myself," Wallace admitted. "He would pull me aside and talk about leadership. We didn't know how good we were. Coach Keeling and his staff are the superstars for motivating us."

Wallace said he didn't see his teammates as being white, black, or Hispanic. "They were just my teammates," he said. "Until I went to Alderson, I hadn't been around Anglos. It was a learning deal for me, too. I never mistreated anyone. I did get to see people not speak to you until I started running for touchdowns and scoring 25 points a game in basketball. Then they didn't mind being my friend. But it was peer pressure for them, too." Wallace continued:

> Coach Keeling was able to make guys feel as if they were important or good. I never thought I was good. I didn't want to be a leader. But I had to give our offensive game plan to the team before every game. Fred White had to cover the defensive game plan. Right before we left for the game, I had to get up in front of the team and say these are the plays we will run. I just wanted to play, but at quarterback you are a leader. I did those things until it became natural. When I was a head coach, I did the same thing. It helped to get in front of your peers. You got to let them know you knew what we were doing. Coach Keeling was able to see things in us that we didn't see in ourselves.

Besides finding out what players would play what position, Keeling had to put together a staff. He said every teacher who was hired was handpicked because of their desire to be at Estacado to make the LISD's first integrated school a success. Keeling did the same thing with his coaching staff, making sure every hire would be the right fit.

His first hire was Delbert Wilson, an Abilene Christian College graduate who had been coaching at Fredericksburg. "Jimmie was at Elgin, and I was in Fredericksburg and aspiring to be a head coach," Wilson recalled. "We had had a lot of success. So I picked up the phone and called Jimmie and asked if I could talk to him about a job. We talked about X's and O's and theory. I was young and fired up about doing something I wanted to do. He hired me. I actually came up in the spring before Estacado opened up. I was the only assistant who came up at that time. That was quite an experience, taking a bunch of ninth graders, a few sophomores from Lubbock High, and maybe a couple from Dunbar. I saw a big change in some of those kids from that spring to the next year. We knew we had a lot of talent. We knew we weren't going to have a lot of size. We didn't have much size in the offensive and defensive lines compared to today, but they could sure run and sure hit."

Wilson, who also served as the head baseball coach, said he had no problem joining the staff at an integrated school. "I don't remember even thinking about that," he stated. "We didn't think about black or white. We just coached kids. We let them know what we expected of them and to be consistent. The one thing I learned from Jimmie more than anything else was that there wasn't anything more important than fundamentals. We never went through a practice that we didn't practice form tackling."

The rest of the staff came in that fall at the start of the 1967–68 school year. Wayne Garner, who had been with Keeling at Tulia a year earlier, rejoined his former boss after one year at Plainview. "I moved around with Jimmie for ten years," said Garner, who coached at Andrews and Lubbock Coronado with Keeling after their time together at Tulia and Estacado. "Jimmie taught me everything I know."

Gene Murrell, a recent graduate of McMurry College where he played for future Baylor University coach Grant Teaff, joined the staff as the backfield coach. R. A. Wade, an assistant basketball coach at Lubbock High the previous year, was named the head basketball coach.

Hollis Gainey, a Colorado City native who had been a member of a world-record-setting 440-yard relay team during his collegiate days at the University of Texas, came to Lubbock from Brenham to be the junior varsity coach and head track coach. "At the time, I was coaching in Brenham," Gainey said. He continued:

> I had two kids who were running in the state cross country meet. I took them to Austin and they ran that morning in the state cross country meet. After the meet, I took them over to the track at UT to give them something to do, and I went over to Rooster Andrews's sporting goods store. I'd known Rooster for quite some time since I went to school in Austin. Rooster said, "Go back there in the back room. There is a coach back there from Elgin, named Jimmie Keeling. I don't think there is anyone back there with him." Jimmie was sitting back there by himself, drinking coffee. I sat down and we visited. He said, "I may be in the running for the head coaching job at a new school in Lubbock. If it works out, would you be interested in coming and being part of the staff?" I told him I would certainly be interested in talking to him about it. End of story. I came to Estacado with Jimmie's staff. We had three great years there. We won a state championship in football and a state championship in track in 1970.

Like Wilson, coaching at an integrated school was no problem for Gainey. "No, no," he emphasized. "Actually at Brenham, that next year Brenham closed its black school and integrated its black students into the Brenham schools. I had no qualms or hesitation about coming to Estacado."

Obviously, Estacado had a lot of talent, according to Gainey. "Jimmie put together a great staff," he added. "These kids came on board in a hurry. They were hungry for some guidance, for some coaching, for some organization. They got after it. The black-white thing was never an issue with the players."

Ricky Mantooth, a former coach at Happy, was hired to coach the ninth grade at Estacado, assisted by Mike Hubbard, who moved up from Hutchinson Junior High. E. G. Nunez, a recent graduate of Texas A&M, was named the trainer at the new school.

Chapter 3

Adjusting to a New School

For the football players—and other students—who came to Estacado in the fall of 1967, it was just a matter of trying to find out how they fit in, not only trying to find a spot on a new football team but also how they would interact socially with students of different ethnic backgrounds.

"My father was prejudiced toward blacks," admitted Joe Rose, a white player who started at center for the Matadors and became one of the leaders of the new school and later a successful businessman. He was elected president of the student body as a senior and served on a committee that helped write the school constitution and select the school colors. But Rose almost didn't attend Estacado.

"My dad was a truck driver, six four, 230 pounds, and thirty-nine years old in 1967," he stated. "He earned a bronze star in the navy during World War II, landing marines on Iwo Jima and at eighteen he earned a second bronze star for landing marines on Okinawa. When they announced the opening of Estacado, we were part of the white flight. We moved to Acuff that summer, and I was supposed to go to Roosevelt [a rural school just outside of Lubbock]."

Rose, however, said he wanted to play football, and he claimed there was no comparison between the Roosevelt High School team and the talent he saw coming into Estacado. So he made a difficult decision. Rose got a job at a supermarket and paid the tuition himself to attend Estacado so he could play football for the Matadors. "It was a great learning experience," he said. "I learned a different culture in the Estacado hallways and being part of the football team. We integrated into each other's cultures."

"My mother, whom my teammates all liked just as they did all of our parents supporting us, attended every single game in 1967 and 1968," Rose continued. "She would travel to the games with Mike Eller's parents, Jack and Marge. Jack was a Lubbock policeman." He added:

> I credit Mr. Eller with finally getting my father to start going to games. And I credit our team, and specifically some of my black teammates, with softening my father's prejudices. Fred White, David Moody, Frank Judie, and James Mosley were always quick to say hello or chat with him. He grew to like these guys and take pride in my being on this team.
>
> My mother Clytie passed away ten years after that 1968 football season at the age of forty-nine. My father Floyd died in the summer of 2016, forty years after Mom. David and Fred visited him in the hospital and at the nursing home. The nurses said he really enjoyed their visits.
>
> What happened to my father was perhaps something that was occurring to others in Lubbock. As they got to know and follow this team, they perhaps grew to admire their accomplishments and accept that they were all just Blue Matadors—and winners.

"Joe Rose was very intelligent," coach Jimmie Keeling said. "He could rally everyone around him. He was a superior leader and a good athlete. As our center, he was in the middle of everything. Remember, we used to huddle in football."

While some white families fled east Lubbock rather than have the children attend Estacado High School, others had a choice and chose to attend the new school.

"I started at Lubbock High School," recalled Melinda Mims Hedgcoth. "When we were told that those of us students that lived in the Cherry Point Addition would have the choice to go to Lubbock High or to the new school, Estacado, a big group of us that went to Alderson Junior High and Lubbock High together chose to go. I wanted to be involved in this new beginning. This was a new school, and we had the opportunity to make the traditions instead of just following them." She continued:

> I was chosen to be on some great committees. I was part of the group that picked our school colors and designed the senior ring. We chose blue and silver for our school colors. Yes, the Dallas Cowboys were an influence. We chose a sterling silver ring that had a phantom "E" in a royal blue stone, and a matador engraved on one side. One of the football players drew the Matador figure that we used, and it was used for everything that had a Matador on it. They may still be using his design. He was quite an artist.

Joe Benson, a black defensive back, said he wasn't nervous about attending the new integrated school. "It was more of a challenge," he said. "I could be just as good as the next guy. You treat me good, I treat you good. You treat me mean, I treat you mean."

When Coach Keeling came in, Benson said, "It was more a thing of let's do something positive."

Fred White, a black linebacker who became an all-stater and the team's defensive leader, noted that the players on the team had a unique relationship. "The athletes set the tone of the school," he emphasized. "We had a positive attitude and got along well. I think the football players had great influence on the school. If the team is disciplined, it helps the school. The coaches tried to teach us to be honorable men."

But even White had his moments. "We realized with Coach Keeling we had someone watching us," White said. "He kicked me off the team during two-a-days. I said I didn't need to listen to them (the coaches), and I got smart with them. I thought I was good enough that they needed me. It was a long walk home, thinking about trying to explain that to my parents."

"I went back and asked to come back," he continued. "Coach Keeling said the guys have to make the decision to allow you to come back. Everyone involved voted to let me come back. All I did was run [when he came back], but it turned my life around. Coach could have said no. Each of our coaches was a great leader. They expected the best out of us. The coaches always planted good seeds."

"Fred was built like a Greek god," Keeling said of White. "He was an intense, fun-loving guy with an infectious laugh. He was a very talented player. He had fun playing football, and he was an unreal leader. Whatever he said to the guys was the law. They would listen to him."

White was easy to spot on the field, too. Defensive coordinator Delbert Wilson said the Matadors wore white helmets, but they didn't have a white helmet to fit White. "So Fred wore a blue helmet, everyone else had a white helmet. It was so we could find him easier," Wilson quipped.

"I don't know if any of these guys realized it, but that school was an experiment in desegregation," observed Benjie Morgan, a black junior varsity player as a ninth grader on the Matadors' first team (his sister, Alpha Morgan, was the 1968 Estacado football sweetheart). "My parents moved to the Thunderbird Addition in Lubbock. We had a choice to go to Struggs Junior High and Dunbar or Alderson Junior High and Lubbock High. Alderson was already integrated—Hispanic, black, and white. It just hadn't been done at the high school level. There were a handful of Hispanics and African Americans going to Lubbock High at the time, but the major experiment was to see how we were all going to come together at this new school. And it worked."

Why did it work?

"I don't know," Morgan admitted. "I was in the ninth grade, so I was there [at Alderson] in the seventh and eighth grade. We all knew each other. We played ball together. We played a lot of sandlot football or street football together in our neighborhoods. There were pockets of racial tension, but for the most part, everyone got along."

Frank Judie, a black fullback for the Matadors, said he attended Struggs until his mother, Dessie White, moved the family to a house on Seventh Street very near Alderson. "I didn't want to go there the next year," Judie recalled. "My mother sat me down and told me to try it for a few weeks. If, after that, I still didn't want to be there, then she would find a way to get me back to Struggs. I had every intention of taking her up on that, but I never did. I had always been a bit of the class clown, having fun with my friends in school. It was sort of expected of me there. However, at Alderson my homeroom elected me as their representative to the student council. That certainly was a new experience for me, to be chosen to represent my classmates in the student government. I began to take my books home with me, study harder, and try to be more serious about school. I didn't want to let them down or fail to earn this new role. I even got myself a briefcase."

"Also, it didn't hurt that Alderson was a totally air-conditioned building, the first school like that back then, I think," Judie recalled. "So I stayed put. It was in the Estacado zone and I would go there next. That is how I got to Estacado."

James Mosley, a black running back who became one of the team's leading rushers, said the new integrated school wasn't that big of an adjustment since he had gone to an integrated elementary school before attending Alderson Junior High. "It was no big change to me," he stated. "Everything was good."

Mosley acknowledged, however, that most people on the outside would probably be shocked to learn that there wasn't racial tension on the team. "They would be surprised," he contended.

"I have talked to my wife about it. I said we never had any kind of problem. Everyone was like brothers. You can see today how we fellowship with each other. It was the same way then."

Why?

"It was a number of things, but I think it was mostly the parents we had," Mosley continued. "All of our parents were grounded and expected us to be the same. My mother was a very religious lady. She lived by the Bible, and I still live by the Bible. She said it taught that everyone—no matter what color or race or religion— is still a person. They are your brother."

Walter Hibbler, a black defensive end, admitted he had some anxiety about going to a new school. "I wasn't sure what to expect," he said. "We had all gone to Alderson Junior High together. Some of us went to the same elementary school. As we were becoming sophomores, we didn't know if we would be going to Dunbar, Lubbock High, or Estacado. Estacado was put into service, so we went there. There were new guys coming in and a new coaching staff, so you didn't know what to expect. We had black, white, and Hispanic teachers. We all melded together. We were all the same family. It really went well for a new school opening."

Would people be surprised there weren't problems?

"Here was our deal," Hibbler pointed out. "We had a tornado or big storm, so we went to the same junior high. There were some problems at first, but after several years, we were all brothers. We were just a big family."

Hibbler credited Coach Jimmie Keeling with making the transition go smoothly. "I didn't know what to expect," Hibbler recalled. "With his leadership and guidance, he made it where the tension wasn't there. With his hand on the steering wheel, Coach Keeling really made a difference. A lot of us came from single-parent families, and Coach Keeling was someone we could go to. I think other students looked at him in that way. He really made a great difference. He used an even hand. He dismissed some of the biggest, meanest kids that we thought we couldn't do without, and he kept some weaker kids. So he was very fair."

Benjie Morgan agreed that Coach Keeling was the key to making the new experiment successful. "He was the kingpin. It started that spring season at Alderson and it moved over to the high school and the JV," Morgan said. "They went 9–1 as sophomores on the JV. He had that spring, the JV season, and then the following spring, doing the same things. The next year they played varsity, they were ready to go." He added:

> One thing that Coach Keeling did was we looked to the game at hand, never looking forward. And we never looked back, the past was history. We always looked forward to the next game. In the spring, we prepared ourselves for the next season. We were the smallest team that went into the playoffs. We were quick. We didn't have pulling guards. We had pulling tackles. It was the speed and quickness of that team that shocked everybody. They were strong, but we had only three guys who weighed over 200 pounds.

"Coach Keeling is a great man, one of the best leaders I have ever seen in my life," added defensive tackle Angel Rodriguez. "Whatever he expected of you, he expected of himself. He was always pushing us and pushing us, but we had a lot of fun and enjoyed it."

"Everything starts at the top," claimed Moody. "We had great coaching. They made us feel like we were part of a family. There wasn't a day that Coach Keeling didn't ask us what we would be doing the rest of our life."

He said the team slogan was "All for One, One for All. A Team That Can't Be Beat, Won't Be Beat."

"When I went to Estacado, I realized I had to compete," continued Moody. "I worked hard to compete. I needed to compete [both on the football field and in the classroom]. I tried not to see color."

"Our line speed was tremendous, except for the white guy in the middle," Rose quipped. "Our 'trap' plays worked well because most of our opponents didn't expect the offensive line to be as quick as the running backs. There were some really good athletes that didn't play, but if they messed the rules up, they were out. We were coached well and molded well. The guys were committed to winning."

He said the leadership came from the coaches, but he praised his black teammates, such as Mosley, Wallace, Moody, White, Hines, Judie, and Hibbler. "They would push you in the weight room," Rose added.

He said much of the melding of cultures occurred on bus rides after the game. "Going to the game, there was silence," Rose stated. "We were thinking about the game. But coming back after we won the game, it was not so serious. There was a lot of singing in the back of the bus, guys doing the hambone and shucking and jiving, and a whole lot of singing."

Rose said they also went to church as a team, attending both black and white churches. "If I had gone to Lubbock High or Roosevelt, I wouldn't have had the experience I had," he concluded. "Sports were just one of the things that I did. It is not just having great talent together; it was also about learning from each other."

J. B. Lemon, a white offensive and defensive lineman, remembers the singing on the bus after games, too. "They were a lively bunch," he laughed. "There was never a dull moment."

"We sang a lot," added Mosley. "Some were better singers than they put out. We enjoyed ourselves. The coaches sat at the front of the bus, and they enjoyed hearing us sing."

Integration meant an adjustment for both the white and black players, according to Lemon. "We never felt that way," he said. "We were like brothers. We never had a problem black or white. The whole time I was in junior high and high school, we never had a problem. I know people would be surprised by that. It was unheard of back in those days, but we never had a problem. It was great. We were together all the time. We were like brothers."

Keeling said he and assistant coach Hollis Gainey hauled kids all over the neighborhood who needed a ride before or after practice. "We had an old clunker of a bus," Keeling recalled. "Hollis and I never took the keys out of the bus. We would go through east Lubbock picking up kids or taking them home."

Tommy Scruggs, a white tight end/punter on the state championship team, said being a part of the team at Estacado made him understand what it was like to be a minority. Scruggs was a newcomer to Lubbock. "We lived in Tulia," he said. "I played under Coach Keeling as a freshman [at Tulia]. But my dad's job was up in the air. We didn't come from perfect homes. So I moved to Lubbock and enrolled in Estacado as a junior."

Because he was a transfer, Scruggs wasn't eligible to play that first season, instead having to wait until his senior year to join the Matadors' varsity squad. He was a running back at Tulia, but moved to tight end at Estacado.

"The football players had the best discipline [among all students at Estacado]," Scruggs stated. "If you were less than exemplary, you had to answer to the coaches."

The players also had to answer to their teammates. The players admitted that the team, unbeknownst to their coaches, had an extrajudicial process in place as well. A few well-respected team leaders were known as "The Judge and the Jury," according to Rose. "If any player was seen or heard disrespecting a teacher or staff member, found not giving 100 percent in practice or games, setting a bad example among students or otherwise bringing disrespect to the team, that person would be told to meet with those guys," he stated. "It would always get worked out. Always."

At the LISD Hall of Honor induction ceremonies in 2013, when the 1968 Matador football team was honored, another former Estacado athlete, Larry Isaac, who went on to play football at Texas Tech and in the National Football League, remembered "The Judge and the Jury."

"By the way, I see a few old friends back there among the '68 Matadors," Isaac said at his individual induction that night. "I was too young to be on that team, but I knew several of them and played with some on our '69 and '70 teams, and 'The Judge and the Jury' was still part of the program."

Maybe one of the more unique newcomers to the Estacado football team was defensive lineman Rudy Beltran. Beltran was married and had dropped out of school. "Coach [E. G. Nunez] said you need to go to school," Beltran said. "Coach Keeling got me a job working as a janitor after school, so I went back to school and graduated."

"He was from Brownfield," Gainey said of Beltran. "They moved to Lubbock, and he was at Lubbock High for one year. Then he transferred over to Estacado. It was after that first season that we played a JV schedule. I was keeping a study hall. Every day that kid would walk in and sit in the front of the study hall, open his books, and do his homework. He was real quiet. That impressed me, and he was a solid, well-built kid. That went on for weeks, and we were in our off season. I talked to him, so he came into off season. We had a room upstairs where we did wrestling. Every kid who challenged him, Rudy threw them off like a matchstick. Gosh, he was strong, and he could move and he was quick. The rest of the story is history. He was a heck of a defensive player."

Of all the kids he coached in his career, Keeling called Beltran "one of the tops in physical toughness."

Keeling said he and his coaching staff visited all the players' homes and got to know their parents. Players and coaches would get together to eat after home games. Mosley said his mother was known for her cooking at those postgame meals. "My mom was an excellent cook, as you can look at me and see," he laughed. "She was a great cook, and she loved to see people eat. She would cook cakes and pies. Most of the team came over to my house to eat after the game. It was a great gathering. There were seven of us—sisters and brothers—so a big crowd wasn't anything different. I think all the guys enjoyed themselves."

Black, brown, and white. The Matadors came together as brothers, not just on the football field but in all facets of life—proof that integration could work. Maybe Moody put it best. "Lives changed for all of us who played for Coach Keeling," he said. "He taught us what life is all about. It is not about X's and O's, but it is how do you change lives."

"We didn't realize how good we could be at the time," Benson concluded. "We played like we had something to prove. We had something that the black community, the whole community, could get behind and be proud of. We [the football players] became the leaders of the school."

Chapter 4

A New Beginning

On the Monday night before the 1967 school year began, the Lubbock Independent School District held a ceremony for the grand opening of Estacado, its newest high school. It was named after the primarily Quaker settlement of Estacado near Lubbock.

Olan Rice, principal of the new school, presided, and James H. Whiteside, president of the Lubbock Independent School District Board of Education, and Nat Williams, LISD superintendent, spoke at the ceremony. The Estacado Concert Choir, directed by Larry Marshall, also performed.

In the story in the *Lubbock Avalanche-Journal* telling of the public grand opening of the new school, however, there was no mention of Estacado being the city's first integrated high school.

Rose Usry, a reporter for the *A-J*, wrote, "Spanish adventurers who first surveyed these vast plains and called them the Llano Estacado could hardly have envisioned the architectural complexities of later centuries and the sophisticated educational facility which in 1967 would encompass some of those acres and bear the colorful and historic name." She continued:

> Estacado High School in northeast Lubbock, the city's new public high school, blueprinted from this century's design for

adequate education to prepare youth to meet the challenges of today and tomorrow, will be open for inspection by the public and formally dedicated at 8 p.m. Monday at its northeast Lubbock location, 1304 Itasca St.

The Lubbock paper said 976 were enrolled for the first day of classes at Estacado.

Lubbock school officials had decided that Estacado, like most new schools in Texas, would play a junior varsity schedule in its first season of competition. Coronado High School had done the same thing when it opened several years earlier. But the decision for Estacado to play a junior varsity schedule that first year came with a debate.

"I thought starting as a JV team was important," former LISD athletic director Pete Ragus recalled. "Mr. [Nat] Williams [LISD superintendent] wanted to jump in and play a varsity schedule that first year. Mr. Williams could be intimidating, but he was the greatest school man I ever worked with. He said, 'You stay with your argument.'"

It was thought that Estacado would be in Class AAAA, the largest classification in Texas at the time, when the University Interscholastic League announced its biannual realignment in 1968, which is why Estacado was able to have spring practice prior to their first junior varsity season. So the Matadors, fielding a team of freshmen and just a handful of sophomores and juniors, played a junior varsity schedule against larger schools, including Lubbock High, Monterey, and Coronado, the city's other AAAA high schools, in the fall of 1967. Most of its games were played on Thursday nights.

Despite playing a JV schedule against larger schools, Estacado quickly served notice that the Matadors were not any ordinary team. They opened the 1967 season with a 58–0 win over the Lubbock High junior varsity.

A week later, Estacado blanked the Coronado JV 18–0 for its second straight shutout of the young season. The *Lubbock Avalanche-Journal* wrote: "Estacado, holding a 6–0 lead at half-time, burst loose for a pair of touchdowns in the third quarter and went on to record its second shutout of the season, 18–0 over the Coronado junior varsity. The Matadors never gave Coronado a chance to score. Fullback James Mosley scored the first touchdown, running thirty-five yards in the second quarter. In the third quarter, Kenneth Wallace scored from the twelve-yard line and James Lester got loose from fifty-five yards and a TD."

Week three brought a third consecutive shutout, and the Lubbock newspaper was starting to take note:

> A fired-up band of Estacado Matadors held the Borger junior varsity to a total of forty-nine yards Thursday while rolling up 249 yards all on the ground in winning their third straight game of the year, 35–0. The Matadors have now gone twelve quarters without allowing their goal line to be crossed and have accumulated 111 points.
>
> James Lester's forty-nine-yard jaunt on Estacado's first offensive try set the tone of the game. Larry Miller added the point after and EHS was on its way, 7–0.
>
> Later in the first period, Kenneth Wallace broke loose for a thirty-two-yard scoring gallop. The PAT failed but the Borger signal-caller was chased out of the end zone for a safety and the Matadors led 15–0 at the close of the initial period.
>
> James Mosley's thirty-yard scamper and Miller's PAT upped the margin to 22–0 midway in the second period. Lester picked off a Borger aerial at the thirty-five and sixty-five yards later Estacado led 29–0. Wallace went five yards in the third quarter to end the scoring. Borger was held to two first downs, while the Matadors picked up thirteen.

The fourth game of the season brought a fourth straight shutout. This time, the victim was Amarillo Tascosa, according to the *Lubbock Avalanche-Journal*:

Using the running of James Lester, plus the passing and running of field general Kenneth Wallace, the Estacado Matadors raced to a 28–0 victory over Tascosa's junior varsity Thursday afternoon in Amarillo.

In running their season ledger to 4–0, the Matadors of Jimmie Keeling chalked up 230 yards over land and sixty more via the air routes while holding the junior Rebs to fifty-two total yards.

Lester scampered seventy-nine yards off tackle in the initial period for the first score. Wallace found Freddie Stephens open for a twenty-seven-yard scoring strike early in the second stanza and then raced forty-one yards on a pass-run option to give the Matadors a 21–0 halftime bulge.

James Mosley's eleven-yard jaunt off tackle in the third quarter concluded Estacado's scoring. Larry Miller kicked all four extra points.

The Matadors had sixteen first downs to just six for the Rebels and hit on four of nine passes and picked off three of Tascosa's twelve attempts. Joseph Benson, David Moody, and Michael McLin recorded the interceptions for Estacado's defense.

"Keeling's troops have now gone sixteen quarters without having their goal crossed while scoring 139 points," the *Lubbock Avalanche-Journal* noted.

Estacado kept it rolling, reeling off six straight wins before losing 16–14 to Amarillo Caprock, a team that Keeling said may have been the weakest it played that first year. The Matadors had given up only one touchdown in the first six weeks before the loss to Caprock. Middle linebacker Fred White missed the Caprock game with an injury, and guard Bobby Lester was out with a broken leg.

"I take credit for that loss," lamented Joe Rose, the team's center. "I snapped the ball over the punter's head. That was our only loss in two years."

The Matadors bounced back from their only loss with a 35–6 win over the Amarillo High junior varsity team. James Mosley scored three touchdowns and Larry Miller added two scores to improve to 7–1. The Lubbock newspaper noted that Estacado had twenty-four first downs, and the Matadors had now scored 292 points while holding their opponents to only 30.

What is football without homecoming, even if it is the first year for a school that is playing a junior varsity schedule?

Sue Evers was crowned as Estacado's first La Matador Reina at halftime of a week nine rout of the Plainview junior varsity team. Student body president Bobby Wells and secretary Donna Wood made the presentation. Evers was presented with a crown and a bouquet of one dozen red roses. The queen's attendants, Debbie Fare and Henri Hicks, were each given a single rose and a plaque.

On the field, the Matadors kept it rolling, as noted in the *Lubbock Avalanche-Journal*:

> Scoring on runs, passes, interceptions and fumbles, Estacado's Matadors blanked the Plainview junior varsity 48–0. The victory hiked the first-year school's record to 8–1 with a game to go.
>
> The Matadors built a 20–0 lead in the first period and didn't let up against Plainview. They held the Bullpups to only eighty-one yards total offense, twenty-four of that on the ground. Estacado raced to 231 yards on the ground and twenty-three in the air and picked up twenty first downs to the visitors' nine.

Joseph Benson followed a short time later with a thirty-eight-yard pass interception score. Larry Miller, who had missed the kick after the first TD, then booted his first of seven extra points. Arthur Morales then added a touchdown on a ten-yard sprint before the quarter ended.

In the second quarter Kenneth Wallace returned a punt sixty-three yards for a score, and Walter Hibbler came back to grab a fumble in the air and race nineteen yards to the goal for a 34–0 halftime advantage.

The Matadors added two more fourth-quarter scores as William Hall took a twenty-three-yard pass from Wallace for a touchdown, and Freddie Stephens plunged over from the one for the final score. Stephens's score was set up by a pass interception. Frank Judie returned the Plainview pass from the thirty-five to the four to set up the TD.

Hall was normally a lineman, but as Keeling explained, "We worked everyone two ways in practice. In the games, we tried to play everyone just one way, but having them work out two ways, it helped with our depth because we wanted our best players on the field."

Estacado then closed out its inaugural campaign with a lopsided victory over the Pampa junior varsity team. It marked the first time that the *Lubbock Avalanche-Journal* used the term "mighty" when referring to the Matadors:

> Utilizing their most ferocious offensive outing of the campaign, Estacado's youthful Matadors flexed their mighty muscles in bouncing Pampa 63–0 at Pampa. In rolling up 401 yards rushing and sixty-four passing, Estacado held Pampa to thirty-three yards in the air and forty-three over land while picking up twenty-one first downs to the junior Harvesters' four, chalking their ninth game against one loss.
>
> James Lester supplied most of the power, scoring on runs of three, fifty-seven and ten yards and returning a kickoff—after a safety—eighty steps for the final touchdown of the day. Larry Miller scampered thirty yards for a score and booted seven PATs. James Mosley raced sixty-one yards for a score, and Freddie Stephens scored on a twenty-seven-yard run.

Chapter 5

No Margin for Error

As the Estacado Matadors began preparation for the 1968 football season, their first while playing a varsity schedule, the rest of the world had seemingly gone crazy.

Earlier that spring, civil rights leader Martin Luther King had been assassinated in Memphis. Then in June, moments after claiming victory in the Democratic primary in California, former attorney general Robert Kennedy, younger brother of assassinated president John F. Kennedy, was gunned down himself in a Los Angeles hotel by Sirhan Sirhan.

The nation was on edge as civil rights demonstrations and protests against the war in Vietnam were dominating the news. But on the practice field, the Matadors and coach Jimmie Keeling were focusing on nothing except making themselves a better football team. Even the most optimistic of the group, however, probably had no idea what the next few months would bring.

Estacado had already received a couple of surprises before the season even began. First of all, Estacado High School's enrollment did not come in as large as initially expected, in part because of white flight from northeast Lubbock as Estacado opened its doors, so the Matadors learned they were put in Class AAA instead of the state's largest AAAA classification when the University Interscholastic League realignment was announced.

Estacado student Suzanne Hallman Smith recalled years later that the demographic housing situation was a primary reason why Estacado's enrollment came in lower than originally anticipated in 1968. "White families sold their nice new homes and left east Lubbock in droves because their children were in the Estacado High School district," Smith stated. "It is a blemish on our society that was felt then and is still evident in many cases. Many of these homes were taken over by HUD (Housing and Urban Development) because the neighborhood had declined. After the 1970 tornado, these same homes were made available to families whose homes had been destroyed, mine included."

The UIL put Estacado in an eleven-team District 3-AAA, meaning the Matadors would not have a nondistrict game. All ten games would count in the district standings. And, to add pressure to each outing, only one team from each district advanced to the playoffs in Texas in 1968. In other words, one loss could bring an end to the season.

Dave Campbell's Texas Football magazine, considered the bible of Texas high school football, didn't foresee what was going to happen, either, predicting the Matadors would finish sixth in the eleven-team district. Sweetwater was the magazine's pick to win the district, followed by Lamesa, Brownfield, Colorado City, Snyder, Estacado, Slaton, Dunbar, Levelland, Littlefield, and San Angelo Lake View.

"Lubbock Estacado posted a flashy 9–1 record a year ago—but playing an informal schedule," the magazine wrote in its annual summer preview edition. "This time around, the rumble is for keeps and even with twenty-two lettermen (ten offensive and ten defensive regulars), the picture is cloudy. However, no doubt surrounds linebacker Fred White (6-1, 178), a connoisseur of contact who could be one of the league's best. He heads up a potentially fine defense. Tackle Mike Martin, linebackers Bobby Lester and David Moody, safety Joe Benson and cornerbacks

Mike McLin and Marvin Turner are other solid talents. WB Tommy Scruggs, TB James Mosley, QB Kenneth Wallace and HB James Lester are the major backfield guns, while Joe Rose, Walter Hibbler, Robert Boykin and Phil Hilton (205) are top offensive lineman."

But *Texas Football* magazine made no mention of the Matadors as it ranked its preseason top ten in Class AAA. Brownwood, the defending state champion, was *Texas Football*'s choice to repeat as state champion. Rounding out its preseason top ten were Mission, Perryton, Waco Moore, Alvin, Henderson, Refugio, Wichita Falls Hirschi, Bridge City, and Dumas. The magazine, however, did correctly pick the champions in four other districts that Estacado would eventually meet in the playoffs—Brownwood (District 4-AAA), Kermit (2-AAA), Henderson (7-AAA), and Refugio (14-AAA).

"We were in an eleven-team district in 1968," assistant coach Hollis Gainey recalled. "Every game was a district game, and there were some good football teams at that time. Brownfield and Lamesa had good football teams, and Sweetwater was an exceptional team. Colorado City had a great football team. Every game was an almost must-win situation. At that time, only one team advanced to the playoffs."

"The coaches had a poster board ladder on the wall in our dressing room," recalled Rose, the team's starting center. "It had 14 rungs to climb—ten with our district games and four for the playoffs and title game. The goal was to win it all."

Mike Eller, a reserve center and long snapper for the Matadors, said the coaches would also put up two posters each week with the team's upcoming opponents' offense and defense strategies on them. "The positions and players' names and photos were across from our names on the depth chart," Eller stated. "The coaches told us, 'Know what they look like. They want to beat you.' That was their message."

"The coaches used to post sports articles from local newspapers of the team we would play," added fullback Frank Judie. "I suppose it was intended to be motivational for the players. Perhaps it was to the others. Where I came out on it was—and I'm not going to say it was racial discrimination exactly—but I read it as very biased against a multiracial football team coming to play them. We were not like them. That really surprised me. I learned more about that tone during the 1967 and 1968 seasons."

Prior to the season, head coach Jimmie Keeling gave each player his own Estacado Matador playbook. Not only did it include plays, but it also listed dates to remember, words of wisdom, advice and guidance, some things that will contribute greatly to "our" success, a list of things to read each week, how players would be evaluated, and rules that everyone should know, including football game rules and team sideline rules.

Keeling did not leave anything to chance.

Estacado opened the 1968 campaign at home against Brownfield, considered one of the leading contenders to win the district title. Brownfield had been 4–6 a year earlier. The Cubs returned quarterback Bobby Craig and six four, 190-pound linebacker Gary Baccus. Longtime *Lubbock Avalanche-Journal* sports writer Walt McAlexander, who later served as a sports information director at both Lubbock Christian University and Texas Tech, came away impressed with the Matadors' defense in a 14–0 win over Brownfield.

"Well, folks, the Estacado Matadors are for real," McAlexander wrote in the next morning's *Avalanche-Journal*. "The Hub City's fledgling grid team made a mistake for each of Lowrey Field's 3,000-plus spectators Friday night in its varsity debut, but a tenacious defense led by Fred White and a breakaway offense sparked by Larry Miller combined for a 14–0 triumph over Brownfield."

The Estacado defense held the Cubs' offensive ground game to a minus-one-yard rushing, and Brownfield completed only three of fifteen pass attempts for ten yards, giving the Cubs a total offensive production of nine yards for the evening.

"With Miller becoming the first Matador to hit the 100-yard rushing mark (117), Estacado rolled up 240 net yards over land and none through the air," McAlexander wrote. "Brownfield was faced with finishing with a minus total for its opening night's work until Roger Roberson hit off tackle for ten yards on the game's final two plays." He went on:

> Up until that time, co-captain White had combined with Frank Judie, Tommy Scruggs, Ronnie Hill, David Moody, Walter Hibbler and James Mosley, just to mention a few, to throw the Cub backs, primarily quarterback Bob Craig, for fifty-two yards in losses.

James Lester scored Estacado's first touchdown on a fifty-one-yard punt return in the second quarter. Mosley added a two-yard run with 3:23 remaining in the third quarter, and Wallace added the two-point conversion on a quarterback keeper for the final score of the evening.

Remember that season-opening score: 14–0 would take an added significance as the season progressed. But for the Matadors, the week one shutout was the first in a ten-step ladder that they planned to climb to the postseason.

Beating the "L's"

The Matadors' next three games were against the "L's": Littlefield, Lamesa, and Levelland. None were any problem for Estacado, which was starting to hit its stride.

Billy Ahrens, a sports writer for the *Avalanche-Journal*, wrote:

> That White "L" in Littlefield looks as though it may stand for "Long." It was a long night for the Wildcats as Estacado

walloped Littlefield 51–0 on the road. David Moody blocked Gerald Haberer's punt and ran it in thirty yards for a touchdown. Larry Miller booted his first of seven extra points and Estacado was off to its second District 3-AAA victory of the season. For the next three quarters, ball-control was the name of the game for Estacado.

The Matadors kept the ball on the ground while rolling up 427 yards. Jesse Lethridge was the top rusher as he gained 165 yards on twelve carries. Lethridge also scored twice on runs of seventy-two and forty yards. Quarterback Wallace scored twice, too, as he rushed for eighty-six yards on just nine carries.

After Moody's touchdown, Estacado kicked off again and the Wildcats lost their first of five fumbles when Lethridge pounced on the ball at the Littlefield fifteen-yard line. Five plays later, with 1:23 remaining in the first quarter, Wallace skirted right end from the fifteen for the touchdown. Miller converted and Estacado led 14–0.

In the second quarter, Miller plunged over from the one, Lethridge raced seventy-two yards, and Wallace danced over from the six for a 35–0 halftime lead.

James Lester scored on a fifty-one-yard run in the third quarter to give the Matadors a 42–0 lead. Then came a safety when the ball was snapped over Haberer's head. Lethridge ended the scoring with a forty-yard touchdown run.

Ahrens, who often used clever analogies in describing the Matadors in his stories in the Lubbock newspaper, wrote about Estacado's third straight shutout victory, a 33–0 win over Lamesa. "Estacado coach Jimmie Keeling billed this game at Lamesa as a 'tough one.' It wasn't," Ahrens wrote. "Lamesa's band did outplay Estacado, however. Estacado's wasn't there. But you don't slug it out, tuba to tuba, to win a game." He continued:

Estacado used the running of fullback Frank Judie to rip Lamesa 33–0 Friday and grab the District 3-AAA lead with a 3–0 record. Judie didn't score a point all evening, but carried the ball thirteen times for 133 yards. A couple of the round-fly's runs set up Estacado's touchdowns.

The Matadors also managed another huge rushing total—366 yards. Passing wasn't anything to talk about, but when a team rushes like that, why pass? Lamesa did put the ball in the air. The Golden Tornadoes attempted thirty passes and connected on twelve for 150 yards. But those goose eggs were still stretched across the Tors' side of the scoreboard when the evening ended.

Estacado's defense scored in the opening minutes. White broke through the Lamesa line to block a Kenny Morton punt at the Tornadoes' twenty-seven-yard line. Moody snatched up the loose ball and rambled in for the score. Miller's extra point try was wide. With ten minutes left in the first quarter, for all practical purposes, the game was over, according to Ahrens.

Wallace scored one of his two touchdowns five-and-a-half minutes later when he danced around right end, and the Matadors led 13–0.

In the second quarter, Estacado did it again with 10:10 remaining. Mosley leaped over from the one and Miller converted the PAT.

The Matadors waited until thirty-five seconds remained in the third period before adding another score. Wallace tossed a forty-nine-yard bomb to Mosley, and the fullback reached the Lamesa one-yard line before he was pushed out of bounds. Wallace plunged over on the next play, and Miller booted his last extra point to make it 27–0.

Miller broke on a slant off left guard and dashed eighty yards for the final Estacado touchdown with 2:05 left in the game.

White, James Lester, and Moody were outstanding on defense. Lamesa could only manage forty-four yards rushing.

"I remember the Lamesa game," defensive end Hibbler recalled. "We were outmanned size-wise. But we had something they didn't have. We had camaraderie."

The next week, Estacado rolled to a 69–0 win over Levelland to improve to 4–0. The state was starting to take notice. The Matadors moved into the state's Class AAA rankings for the first time, debuting at No. 10 following the Levelland win.

Wallace opened the scoring with an eighteen-yard TD pass to Mosley. Wallace, who also hit Mosley on a forty-nine-yard touchdown aerial to open the second half, returned two punts for touchdowns, too, against the Lobos, a fifty-nine-yarder in the second quarter and a sixty-five-yard return in the third period.

Judie, Larry Miller, Lethridge, Benson, and backup quarterback Jesse Bozeman also had rushing touchdowns in the Matadors' lopsided victory.

The Estacado defense also came up big. Besides posting a fourth straight shutout, it scored a safety and added a touchdown when Benson returned a fumble recovery eight yards for another score.

"I remember the Levelland game," Wallace recalled. "We were beating them bad. It was like a Mash unit. They were hauling kids off the field. I felt bad. That is how intimidating our defense was, how hard we were hitting them. They wouldn't get up. I hated that."

Despite entering the poll for the first time, state rankings were not top priority for the Matadors players. Next up was the "biggest" game of the year for city bragging rights.

Larry Miller runs the ball against Dunbar behind the blocking of Robert Hines (72), Frank Judie (31), Joe Rose (50), and James Mosley (32). Photo credit *EHS Echo*.

Fullback Frank Judie turns the corner on a run against Dunbar. Photo credit *EHS Echo*.

Quarterback Kenneth Wallace keeps the ball against Slaton. Photo credit *EHS Echo*.

James Mosley has the ball stripped away as he runs against Slaton. Photo credit *EHS Echo*.

James Mosley finds a hole against the tough Sweetwater defense. Photo credit *EHS Echo*.

James Mosley scored the game's only touchdown on a dive against Sweetwater behind the blocking of Freddie Stephens (84) and Robert Hines (72) to clinch the district championship. Photo credit *EHS Echo*.

The mayor of Lubbock reads a proclamation from the city at the pep rally before the bi-district game against Brownwood. Photo credit *EHS Echo*.

The Estacado line opens a hole against Brownwood. Photo credit *EHS Echo*.

Center Joe Rose (50) and linebacker Fred White (83) converse on the sideline in the Matadors' bi-district win over Brownwood. Photo credit *EHS Echo*.

Estacado players celebrate after beating defending state champion Brownwood in the first round of the playoffs. Photo credit *EHS Echo*.

The Estacado sideline as they watch the Matadors beat Kermit in the area round. Photo credit *EHS Echo*.

Quarterback Kenneth Wallace turns the corner on a keeper in the semifinal win over Henderson. Photo credit *EHS Echo*.

Fred White holds the trophy after the Matadors beat Henderson to move on to the state championship game. Photo credit *EHS Echo*.

The Estacado defense swarms to tackle a Refugio ball carrier in the state title game victory. Photo credit *EHS Echo*.

Estacado coach Jimmie Keeling shows Dallas Cowboy legend Bob Lilly the state championship trophy. Lilly was the guest speaker at the team's football banquet following the season. Photo credit *EHS Echo*.

Alpha Morgan was named the football team's sweetheart in 1968. Photo credit *EHS Echo.*

The 1968 homecoming royalty was (*left to right*) Carole Knowles, homecoming queen Thelma Moore, and Susie Hefner. Photo credit *EHS Echo.*

Chapter 6

Bragging Rights

Perhaps no game meant more to the Matadors, especially the African American players, than their week five cross-town match against Lubbock Dunbar. In most cases the players knew each other. They had grown up together and would have been teammates at Dunbar if the Lubbock school district hadn't opened Estacado High School a year earlier.

"That was the game of the century (at least for the east side of Lubbock)," quarterback Kenneth Wallace emphasized. "Dunbar went to the playoffs in 1967 and lost to eventual state champion Brownwood. They had speed to match us. I was playing against guys that I had gone to school with."

"I knew all those guys," defensive end Walter Hibbler added. "They were always ragging me because I went to Estacado and my girlfriend went to Dunbar. I was player of the week in that game."

And what happened to the girlfriend?

"I married her," Hibbler laughed. "She made me an honest man. She gave me two sons. We have been married since 1981, and she is still putting up with me."

Estacado's defense was obviously ready for a game against its cross-town rival long before the game itself arrived, according to backup quarterback/defensive back Daniel Johnson. "During practice that week, Coach Keeling asked the team, 'Are you ready?'

We responded, 'Yeah, Yeah, Yeah!'" recalled Johnson. "I was the scout team quarterback, running Dunbar's plays. I broke a couple of times down field. Coach Keeling got with the defense. The next time I broke down field, David Moody, Fred White, or someone else hit me. I couldn't breathe. I was taken out of practice. While on the sideline, here comes someone with a shoulder injury, another with an ankle injury, and a guy with a split helmet. Shortly afterward, here comes a second and third guy with split helmets. Coach Keeling called the team together and then sent the team to the house. I guess he knew we were ready. At the rate we were going, he wouldn't have had any players left after practice to play Dunbar. For the rest of the week, there was no live hitting."

Ronald "Bubba" Kinner, who played wide receiver and cornerback for Dunbar, downplayed the rivalry, however. "A lot of my teammates and a lot of people in our community probably thought of it more as a rivalry than I did," he said. "I knew those guys growing up. I'd known Ken Wallace since we were four years old, and we were pretty tight through the eighth grade. To me, it was a big game against another school that happened to have a lot of guys on their team that I knew a lot about. I've always thought it was a real privilege to have played against that team. They were one of the greatest high school football teams in Texas, then and now. We had a good team that year, but they were better."

But John Mayse, a guard and center on the Dunbar team who later spent more than twenty years coaching high school football, said there was no doubt the Estacado-Dunbar matchup was a rivalry game. "Big time! It hurt when we lost it, and I regret it to this day," Mayse stated. "Because we had all grown up together, that is why it meant so much to some of us players and many in the community. I lived across the street from James Mosley. We called him 'Rock' back then because he was The Man, offense or defense. Marvin Turner and Walter Hibbler played with us, too, before high school. We should have all been playing together then, too. We had a high school reunion recently. My wife and

I sat next to Walter Hibbler and his wife, who graduated from Dunbar. We had a good time together. The state championship meant more to the Estacado guys that year, but that game is what I will remember about that year."

It was standing-room only for a Saturday night showdown at Lowrey Field between the two teams. But, as Billy Ahrens wrote in the Sunday morning *Lubbock Avalanche-Journal*, the historic matchup turned out to be another shutout for the Estacado defense: "Some 18,000 eyes saw a defense more punishing than Sing Sing Saturday evening at Lowrey Field. It was Estacado's and Dunbar saw it all too well," Ahrens wrote. "It was New Year's Eve to Estacado. It was a funeral to Dunbar. Estacado buried Dunbar 26–0 and moved even further into the District 3-AAA lead with a 5–0 record. And the Matadors are still unscored on."

Estacado's offensive machine kept rolling, too. The Matadors rushed for 362 yards and went to the airways for forty-two more yards in ripping Dunbar's defense to shreds. Sophomore Jesse Lethridge carried the ball sixteen times for ninety-six yards to lead Estacado's ground game. Fullback James Mosley piled up ninety-two yards on twenty carries.

A defense led by Hibbler and middle linebacker Fred White punished the Panthers all evening. A. G. Perryman, Dunbar's powerful 215-pound fullback, could only manage seventeen yards on ten carries. Dunbar, now 2–1–1, picked up four first downs, and two of those came from frantic passing in the final period.

Perryman, who later earned a scholarship to the University of Oklahoma, had been an all-state guard and defensive lineman in 1967, but in 1968 he was moved to fullback. He finished the season with 1,083 yards rushing, scored 136 points, and was named the *Lubbock Avalanche-Journal* Player of the Year. Defensive back Joe Benson said Perryman was a load to handle. "Dunbar had a big running back, and I was a little guy," Benson recalled. "They said he could run right over me, but I knocked him down. That is what I remember, knocking those guys down."

Benson, who later became an all-American at Sul Ross State, set the Estacado school record with seven interceptions as a junior and eight more as a senior, but he never got a "pick six," an interception returned for a touchdown. "No, but I kept a whole lot of other guys from getting touchdowns," he claimed. "If I'm not going to get one, you are not going to get one. There was never a touchdown pass thrown over me."

Dunbar as a team had minus-two yards rushing against the Estacado defense, although the Panthers came up with a forty-two yards in the air to at least end the game with positive total yardage.

"In the opening minutes of the game, Estacado moved the ball with probably more authority than Ho Chi Minh has," Ahrens wrote. "The Matadors started on their twenty and moved to the Dunbar fifteen. From that point, facing a fourth-and-four situation, quarterback Kenneth Wallace faded back to pass when cornerback Ronald Kinner came in to take it off Wallace's arm. The drive took up six and a half minutes and before anyone realized it, the first quarter ended."

"Estacado finally decided it didn't like the look of goose eggs on the scoreboard," Ahrens continued. "Near the end of the second period, Dunbar punted on third down, but nobody was back to receive it for Estacado. It was a thirty-nine-yard boot to the Estacado forty-eight-yard line. Five plays later, after Wallace hit tight end Tommy Scruggs with a thirty-six-yard pass to the Dunbar five, Mosley broke the ice with a three-yard scoring jaunt."

"Coach used me at corner sometimes, and I was to rush the quarterback from the outside," Dunbar's Kinner explained. "It worked that time when I took the ball away from Kenneth [Wallace]. Later, Coach had me in when Kenneth threw a long one to their tight end. I had let him get past me, and I didn't catch him until he got to our five."

Larry Miller kicked the extra point after Mosley's touchdown, and it was 7–0 with 1:48 remaining in the first half. Mosley came back to score again with 5:54 left in the third quarter. This time it was a one-yard plunge and the Matadors held a 14–0 advantage.

Estacado added two more touchdowns in the final period, including a twenty-six-yard run up the middle by fullback Frank Judie. "Of course, a lot of them knew us and we knew many of them," Judie noted, and he continued:

> Sometimes the boundary between Dunbar and Estacado ran right down the middle of a neighborhood street. They had good players. One, A. G. Perryman, was a big fullback on offense with a hard-running style like James Mosley. He played middle linebacker and sometimes defensive tackle on defense, too. He gained a lot of yards as a running back that season, but not against us. Our defense hit him hard every time whether he had the ball or not. I think we banged him up a bit, but you still had to respect his size and abilities.
>
> On defense, he was the middle linebacker, and I heard him shout out, "Watch Judie, watch Judie!" Coming from him that sounded odd to me, but I guess he meant that where I was going, the tailback would probably follow.

The *Echo*, Estacado's school newspaper, made humorous note of the victory over their crosstown rival Dunbar: "Ghosts at Lowrey Field?" the *Echo* wrote. "Yes, there really were ghosts at Lowrey Field, the ghosts of the Matadors. Two weeks ago, the Dunbar Panthers had a funeral in their pep rally for the Matadors." The article continued:

> After the reading of the obituary and several other things that make up a Matador funeral, they buried the Matadors. To the surprise of the Panthers, the spirit of the Matadors returned in the blue jerseys and silver helmets.

After three hours of downs, punts, penalties and tackles, the Matadors returned to their ghostly castle with a score of twenty-six and the Panthers returned to their haunted house with zero.

Ghostly Matador Freddie Stephens says, "It was a spooky victory, but it was fun."

Dunbar would go on to finish third in District 3-AAA with only the loss to Estacado and a 6–6 tie with Sweetwater (the Mustangs were actually declared the winner of that game based on penetrations of the twenty-yard line, which was how the University Interscholastic League broke ties in 1968).

Estacado was now 5–0 and halfway toward its goal of a district championship.

Chapter 7

But We Won

How can you win a sixth straight game, score seventy-three points, and still be upset? Surprisingly, that was the story in a week six rout of San Angelo Lake View. The Estacado football team was upset because the Chiefs actually scored a touchdown against them. For the first time in six weeks, the Matadors' defense had finally given up a score.

Billy Ahrens made note of the end to Estacado's remarkable defensive streak in the *Lubbock Avalanche-Journal*:

> As the sun slowly set in the North, San Angelo Lake View scored a touchdown against Estacado. Impossible? At least half of it is true. When Lake View scored on the Matadors, it set one record. But Estacado came back to set another—73 points worth.
>
> It was crazy, man, crazy. It should be anytime the final outcome is 73–6. At the time of this writing on a Saturday afternoon at Lowrey Field, Estacado fans, which are strong in voice and not in number, are chanting, "We're Number One."
>
> Estacado isn't the Number One team in Texas. It's Number Seven. But the Matadors finally lose the distinction of being the only unscored-on congregation in the state.
>
> So, after a battle billed to be worse than that skirmish General Custer had, Estacado runs its District 3-AAA record to 6–0. Lake View falls deeper into the cellar at 0–6. It was one

of those games when Estacado scored nine touchdowns and had nine first downs.

Then came the inevitable. With Estacado leading 33–0, Lake View, after taking the kickoff, started at its thirty. On the Chiefs' second play, halfback Jimmy Don Williams was issued the ball on a simple draw over right guard. He found a hole, dashed through it and broke to the right and the sidelines. The Estacado bench couldn't believe it. They knew what was coming. And there went Williams sixty-seven yards into the end zone.

33–6. And every Matador looked as though he had just received his notice to report for a draft physical. But there were better times for Estacado.

"It was the first time we had been scored on," defensive coordinator Delbert Wilson said. "Fred White was in the game on defense, and they broke one sixty-seven yards for a touchdown. Fred walked off Lowrey Field. I tried to talk to him, but he wouldn't even look at me. One of the best decisions I made was to not talk to him. It took him about a week to get over that. Coach [Jimmie] Keeling has often said that he was glad that it happened [Lake View scored]. We had a big lead, and he was glad that happened then and not in a 6–0 game. We got that out of the way."

"We were unscored on," defensive line coach Wayne Garner added. "I was coaching the defensive tackles, and my primary job was to stop the trap. I was in the press box that day, and I thought I was going to be fired after I saw Lake View break the trap. I was twenty-six years old, and I wasn't confident of my stability."

Despite giving up a score for the first time this season, there were plenty of big-play offensive highlights for the Matadors. Quarterback Kenneth Wallace scored on the second play of the game when he skirted right end from forty-eight yards out. Larry Miller then kicked his first of three conversions. Later,

Miller was kicked out of the game, Ahrens noted, and J. B. Lemon took over the kicking duties.

Jesse Lethridge, who rushed for 144 yards on nine carries, scored on the next possession on a forty-six-yard run. Then Miller scored on a seventy-five-yard sweep around left end.

As the second quarter opened, Wallace scored on an eighty-two-yard punt return, and James Mosley made it 33–0 on a four-yard run.

Then came the Lake View six-pointer.

Fullback Frank Judie came back with a seventy-yard TD, a run that epitomized one of the real strengths of the Estacado team. "I got through the line of scrimmage and saw a clear field open for a long run," Judie reflected. "I turned it up and was running as fast as I could. When I looked left and right, I found our two tackles running stride for stride with me and not even breathing hard. Robert Hines and William Hall were escorting me to the end zone. Who would expect that? How do you prepare your team to play offensive tackles with that kind of speed?"

"I have a friend I coached with later at Waco Midway who had played at Brownwood against us," added Garner, who also coached the offensive line for the Matadors. "He said it was astounding to him that Hall played offensive tackle, and then he saw him in track that spring and Hall was running a 9.8 in the 100."

Judie's touchdown run was followed by Lethridge's forty-yard score. In the third stanza, Mosley ripped off a forty-three-yarder thanks to the blocking of Tommy Scruggs and William Hall. Freddie Stephens hauled in a twenty-one-yard scoring toss from Wallace, and Daniel Johnson went in from the four to end the third-quarter scoring.

"With 9:25 remaining in the game, Johnson tossed a seventeen-yarder worth six points to Marvin Turner, who in turn ripped off his helmet to expose a grin wider than the Mississippi River," Ahrens wrote. "When the stats were totaled, Estacado finished with 526 yards rushing. Besides Lethridge's 144, Miller rolled up ninety-three yards on five carries, Judie got eighty-six and Mosley totaled seventy steps. Estacado's defense, led by Fred White, Walter Hibbler, David Moody, Robert Boykin. Rudy Beltran and Mike McLin, gave up 70 yards rushing and three first downs in the opening half."

Even if they weren't on the football team, many in the student body were involved with the success of the Matadors. For example, Melinda Mims Hedgcoth, who was a member of the varsity choir, said she was involved in so many different ways. She was on the team that wrote the school song.

"I can still sing every word, and it still gives me chills," she stated. "I didn't make cheerleader, but I wanted to be part of it all. The head cheerleader was my best friend during that year and delegated me plenty to do. I helped come up with a slogan each week for the game. Glenda Rankin, who is a great artist, and I made a run-through sign with the slogan on it. We also held it at the games for the team to run through. Our whole group would do skits and pick the yells for every pep rally."

Mims Hedgcoth said she wanted to decorate the locker room for every game to pump the guys up. "I decided to make twelve full-sheet white construction paper signs that had #1 in blue glitter and 12 half-size signs that also had #1 in blue glitter and stick them up randomly," she said. "There was one time I slipped up. I had finished decorating the locker room and was standing outside by the bus when Fred White came running out in a panic holding one of the large signs. I asked what was wrong, and he told me there were thirteen signs instead of the regular twelve. Well, it happened that a lot of football players are superstitious. I had to dispose of the thirteenth sign immediately. I counted them twice after that."

Chapter 8

Seven Down, Three to Go

As the Estacado football team continued to roll over its opponents, the players were seemingly oblivious to the outside world that was spinning out of control. Not only were events of gigantic stride occurring daily, weekly, and monthly that would continue to shape the country's political, judicial, economic, and cultural identity for years to come, but also the national and world news was coming into everyone's home in Lubbock and across the United States.

The news would no longer wait for a morning paper, but instead was broadcast nightly on television, often with on-scene reports and live camera footage. The deadliest years of the Vietnam War were 1967 and 1968, and the carnage of bombings, battles, and atrocities were regular features for a war-weary public to witness. The growing antiwar movement would spread from student protests on college campuses to the civil rights movement. Civil rights protests would grow and increasingly be met with violent response or violence from frustrated or impatient supporters.

In Lubbock, the local school board, in a decision meant to appease the federal government's and court's demands for full public school integration, voted to build a new (fifth) high school in east Lubbock as the first fully integrated high school in the city. Did these prominent civic-minded men with good intentions make some short-sighted decisions resulting in unintended long-term consequences? Perhaps a decision to fully integrate LISD instead of only one school would have been the right thing to do for the city and the school system. East Lubbock, a new high-growth area for Lubbock housing and retail business development at the time, would never recover, and their decisions only delayed school integration in Lubbock.

Of course, the fourteen- to eighteen-year-old students who would attend the new school in the fall of 1967 didn't understand the circumstances that led to the new school. The majority of these students knew each other from their neighborhoods, churches, and elementary and middle schools. Some of them would attend the new school in 1967, but then move with the family out of the school's enrollment area, or even out of the Lubbock district entirely, before the start of the 1968 school year.

Members of the Matadors team were more than just football players. They were also active in the classroom. Suzanne Hallman Smith, a student at Estacado, recalled her English class in the fall of 1968. "The class was reading *The Adventures of Huckleberry Finn*," she said. "Ms. Worley assigned Larry Miller to read the part of Jim, the runaway slave. After a few very shy and nervous attempts, he finally followed her example of the style she expected him to use. He was fabulous with a drawl and dialect you would expect to hear. He played the part so well, even down to the 'hand jive' slapping on his legs as he read a portion of the story when he and Huck were singing one night at the campfire. Larry had been the quiet guy in the class until Ms. Worley pulled him out, and he began to enjoy English class. The entire class was blown away with Larry Miller's 'hidden gift.' We knew him as a powerful football player, but performing like he did? No way!"

Another student, Janet Stoudt Short, said the memories she had as a girl saw more problems with how kids were raised to treat others than the actual students themselves. "The students that made up the core student body were mostly willing to make Estacado a great school because so many adults from other parts of town were determined it would fail and be dangerous," Short reflected. "There is one choir program we had at night that I remember caused some parents to be unhappy about. At the end of the program, the choir sang 'Bridge over Troubled Water' and held hands across the stage with white, black, and Hispanic students together. Some of the audience wasn't seeing just kids holding hands. This choir program was probably the closest any of us got to a protest about race. We were friends and had made school a safe place for most."

On the football field, however, the focus was simply trying to win another game and keep alive the dream of going to the play-offs. Estacado followed up the 73–6 rout of San Angelo Lake View with another lopsided victory, a 60–6 win over Slaton, a team that had been 7–2 in 1967 in Class AA before moving up to AAA in 1968. Midweek, following the win over Slaton, Bill Ahrens wrote a column in the *Lubbock Avalanche-Journal* titled "Seven Down, Three to Go" as he put the Matadors' numbers in perspective.

"It is getting to the point where one doesn't recognize a football team by its colors. You recognize a team by the type of offense it runs," Ahrens pointed out in his colorful style. "It's not hard to tell which one is Estacado." He wrote:

> After a 60–6 victory over Slaton the past weekend, the road to that District 3-AAA crown is getting shorter. The Matadors now must face Snyder, Colorado City and finish with Sweetwater in a game that will surely not be for the faint-heart type.
>
> Estacado has now won seven of its district wars. Three more will mean a shot at the state title. . . .
>
> The real hot potato is Estacado. Some Triple A teams are about as exciting as a Saturday night in Moran, Texas. Estacado is different. The statistics reveal the power of the Quirt Avenue

school. The Matadors have rolled up 328 points. Opponents have scored 12. In seven games, the opposition has rushed for 315 yards and collected 267 via the airways.

But stats aren't as exciting as the players. The Matador defense, led by 190-pound middle linebacker Fred White, is rougher than a three-day hangover. Estacado's backfield has more depth than the Grand Canyon.

Quarterback Kenneth Wallace runs a roll out with authority. He's a 10.2 man. Tailback Larry Miller, a towering 175-pounder who hits 10.5, delights in running over body structures. Wingback James Mosley carried his 205 pounds in 10.5 speed. Fullback Frank Judie, the shortest man in the world standing under a helmet, moves his 185 pounds over 100 yards in 10.7.

Estacado coach Jimmie Keeling says they all have better speed for thirty or forty yards.

Then comes the second team. Tailback Jesse Lethridge runs a 9.7. So does wingback Joe Benson. James Lester has turned in a 9.7 also. Third-team tailback Marvin Turner is a 10-flat individual.

Estacado's defense held opponents scoreless for five games. Then came whipping-boy San Angelo Lake View. The Chiefs scored. Last week, Slaton scored. It's not that the Matadors' defense is turning to slop. As Keeling put it, "It just had to happen sometimes."

The fast backs, a stout defense and a talented coaching staff have put Estacado in the state rankings. It is something to be proud of, but not a word is said about it at Estacado.

"They know it, but they don't talk about it," says Keeling. "Oh, I'm sure they are proud."

Once a team is regarded as one of the best in state, what affect does it have? "Once you are up there, you want to stay there," answers Keeling.

"The parents in our community were special," Mosley noted. "When we had that run, especially when no one was scoring on us and we were running up big wins, we made a ladder, and every time we won we would fill in a rung. We didn't want to stumble until we got all fourteen of them."

The Matadors were halfway up the fourteen-rung ladder of success.

Chapter 9

Setting the Table

As Estacado headed down the home stretch of the 1968 season, rolling over opponents by lopsided scores, what did opposing teams think about the Matadors?

"The only thing I knew about Estacado prior to the game was the explosive speed illustrated by their game films," recalled Colorado City running back Dan Steakley, who went on to play running back for the University of Texas Longhorns. "Having run against them in track the year before, I knew we were in for a huge challenge."

Several of the teams that Estacado played were dealing with integration and the changing times of 1968, too. "I was not aware that Estacado was the first integrated school in Lubbock," Steakley said. "My father, Dr. H. Jene Steakley, was a school board member during the mid- and late 1960s and was a huge advocate for integration. My father was a greatly admired dentist in Colorado City for over thirty years due to his dental expertise along with his activities on the school board, Lions Club, First Baptist Church, and numerous other civic and church-related causes. As I recall, Colorado City ISD officially integrated in 1965, my freshman year in high school. Though there were concerns, to my knowledge, our small town did not experience any integration problems, racial problems, or distractions. We were only spectators of the '1968 turbulent times.'"

Matadors at the 1992 reunion of the Estacado state championship team were (*left to right*) Walter Hibbler, Robert Hines, James Mosley, Fred White, Marvin Turner, Tommy Scruggs, J. B. Lemon, Mike Eller, Benjie Morgan, Joe Rose, and Kenneth Wallace. Photo courtesy of Kenneth Wallace.

A large group of players from Estacado's 1968 state championship team, cheerleaders, and other students gathered for a reunion in 1992. Photo courtesy of Kenneth Wallace.

Among those attending the thirtieth anniversary reunion of Estacado's state championship team in 1998 were (back row, *left to right*) Coach Hollis Gainey, Coach Gene Murrell, Fred White, David Moody, Tommy Scruggs, Walter Hibbler, Robert Hines, William Hall, Kenneth Wallace, (front row) Rudy Beltran, manager Melvin Mitchell, Joe Rose, Coach Jimmie Keeling, James Mosley, Avance Green, Mike Eller, and Frank Judie. Photo courtesy of Kenneth Wallace.

Matadors gathering for a reunion in 2016 at Tommy Scruggs's home included Angel Rodriguez, Frank Judie, James Lester, Rudy Beltran, J. B. Lemon, Coach Jimmie Keeling, Tommy Scruggs, Homer Morse, Fred White, David Moody, Walter Hibbler, Joe Rose, Kenneth Wallace, Jesse Lethridge, and Daniel Johnson. Photo courtesy of Linda Scruggs.

Hollis Gainey, Jimmie Keeling, and Gene Murrell, coaches on the 1968 state championship team, attended the 1998 reunion of Estacado's state title team. Photo courtesy of Kenneth Wallace.

Attending the funeral for teammate Avance Green were Fred White, David Moody, Joe Rose, Walter Hibbler, Mike Eller, Frank Judie, Kenneth Wallace, and James Mosley. Photo courtesy of Joe Rose.

Attending Estacado teammate Avance Green's funeral were (*left to right*) Mike Eller, Fred White, Tommy Scruggs, David Moody, Walter Hibbler, Frank Judie, Joe Rose, and Kenneth Wallace. Photo courtesy of Joe Rose.

In 2004, Jimmie Keeling was honored in Abilene where he was coaching at Hardin-Simmons University for his fiftieth year of coaching. Estacado Matadors attending the event at the Abilene Civic Center were (*left to right*) David Moody, Tommy Scruggs, Fred White, Coach Jimmie Keeling, Joe Rose, Kenneth Wallace, Frank Judie, and Mike Eller. Photo courtesy of Kenneth Wallace.

While the transition to the changing world continued, the Matadors had two more hurdles to clear on the football field before a regular-season finale at Sweetwater that was shaping up to be a monumental one-game winner-take-all showdown for the district title and a postseason berth.

But standing in the way first were the Snyder team and Steakley's Colorado City team. Keeling made sure the Matadors weren't looking past either the Tigers or the Wolves.

Billy Ahrens wrote about the road whitewash of Snyder in the next morning's *Lubbock Avalanche-Journal*: "The Estacado energetics pulled that deadly sword out of its scabbard Friday evening in Snyder," he penned. "That sword was Estacado's steam-rolling offense and slicked into Snyder, 54–0. The same old names showed up once again in the Matadors' scoring summary. James Mosley and Kenneth Wallace each scored twice to highlight the offense." Ahrens continued:

And when the cutting was finished, Estacado had carved out 399 yards rushing and forty-seven passing. For the first time this season, however, not one Matador went over the 100-yard rushing barrier. But it didn't make a difference as Estacado collected its eighth straight District 3-AAA win. Snyder tumbled to a 2–5 record.

Estacado's defense again left an opponent with a mini-rushing total. The Tigers could only muster twenty-seven yards rushing, but saved face with 103 yards through the airways.

Snyder fullback David McGinnis (who later played football at Texas Christian University, was head coach of the Arizona Cardinals, and is now an assistant coach for the Los Angeles Rams), better known for his running abilities, snagged four aerials for eighty-eight yards. The Matadors' defense led by middle linebacker Fred White, held Snyder to six first downs, and four of those came in the latter stages of the game.

"As the game opened, it didn't take long for Estacado to make believers of the 3,000 Tiger fans," Ahrens wrote. "The second time Snyder had the ball, it wasn't able to move and a punt was on the agenda." He went on:

> Tiger Steve Holder took the snap to punt, but the body structure of James Mosley was there to block it. White picked it up at the Snyder fifteen and hustled into the end zone. Miller kicked and it was 7–0 with 5:36 left in the first quarter.

Moments later, Snyder punted again. Estacado moved from its own thirty-nine to the Snyder one-yard line in seven plays. With twenty-three seconds remaining in the first period, Mosley blasted over from the one and Miller converted. The longest gain in the drive was an eighteen-yard pass from Wallace to White.

The Matadors didn't let up in the second quarter. With 10:10 remaining, Miller scored on a one-yard run. On the ensuing kickoff, the kick fell short and Robert Boykin pounced on the ball at the Tiger thirty-eight. Six plays later, fullback Judie bulled over from the two and Miller booted the conversion to make it 28–0.

With 5:11 left before intermission, Jesse Lethridge broke off tackle on a thirty-eight-yard scoring jaunt. That made it 34–0.

Estacado took the third-period kickoff and moved methodically down the field in twelve plays, with Wallace scoring on a one-yard keeper. The drive took five minutes and twenty-two seconds.

Mosley, who added a thirty-seven-yard TD run, ended the night with ninety yards on fourteen carries. Lethridge mustered up sixty-seven yards on six assignments.

"The Matadors then showered, dressed and put that sword back into the scabbard. But it will probably come out again next Friday for Colorado City," Ahrens noted.

Prior to the Colorado City game, the football team received blue blazers, as noted in the *Estacado Echo*: "Forty blue figures invaded the hall of EHS two weeks ago as the Matador football team proudly displayed their new blazers. The royal blue blazers were ordered last May for the boys to wear to pep rallies and out-of-town games. The single-breasted blazers sport silver buttons and a matador insignia on the lapel. The adult booster club is undertaking a number of activities to help raise money that will pay the $1,200 for the blazers. Among these activities are the sale of bumper stickers and corsages for the homecoming game tomorrow."

Colorado City proved to be no match for the Matadors.

"If Estacado was looking ahead to Sweetwater, Colorado City should be grateful," Ahrens wrote in the Sunday *Avalanche-Journal*. "The malicious Matadors, behind the running of James Mosley and Jesse Lethridge, poured it on the Wolves 42–0 on a brisk, autumn Saturday night at Lowrey Field. The Matadors rolled up 366 yards rushing and hit on two passes for 67 yards for a 433-yard offense." Ahrens continud:

> Estacado's defense, which has held the other side to two touchdowns this season, gave up eighty-five yards rushing. On Colorado City's last possession, Steakley, who played both ways for the Wolves, got thirty-seven of those eighty-five yards.

Lethridge scored a pair of touchdowns on runs of fifteen and twenty-five yards against Colorado City. The sophomore totaled seventy-five yards rushing on eight attempts.

Estacado rolled up 247 yards rushing in the first half. But the defense scored the Matadors' first touchdown.

After Colorado City picked up a first down in three plays, quarterback Keaton Grubbs went to the air, but Estacado's Marvin Turner picked it off at the Wolves' twenty-eight and headed home to make it 6–0 with 10:30 left in the quarter. Larry Miller booted the conversion.

Then Miller scored one of his own. Starting at its thirty-eight, Estacado moved to the Colorado City seventeen in seven plays. With 2:06 left in the first period, Miller skirted left end on a pitchout and converted to make it 14–0.

"Next scorer was rip and roaring 138-pound tailback Jesse Lethridge," Ahrens added. "He weaved his way up the gut from fifteen yards out and Miller kicked to give Estacado a 21–0 lead with 10:38 remaining in the opening half. Mosley, who rushed for 105 yards in the first half, finished out the second-quarter scoring with a forty-eight-yard, high-stepping jib with 3:49 left. Of course, Miller kicked the point after."

During halftime activities, Thelma Moore was crowned homecoming queen. The *Lubbock Avalanche-Journal* noted that Moore was a senior and drum major for the Matador band. Her court included Carole Knowles, a senior cheerleader, and Susie Hefner, head cheerleader. Alpha Morgan was also presented as the team's 1968 Football Sweetheart.

"I was honored to be selected as the Football Sweetheart," Alpha Morgan Heggie recalled years later. "I remember that we had an outstanding team and an unbelievable season, which gave the school and student body a lot of inspiration. The winning attitude and camaraderie of the players and their families helped foster a bond between different ethnic groups and socioeconomic backgrounds in school and in the community. The team was a rallying point that everyone supported. It was awesome. I also believe the academics, teachers, and coaches prepared students to compete at the next level in college and in the workforce."

After graduation from Estacado, Morgan Heggie attended Rice University, was a member of the cheerleading squad there for two years, and earned two degrees. Since then she has enjoyed a career as a certified public accountant in both the public and private sectors. She and her family live in Houston.

Homecoming queen Thelma Moore, now Thelma Daniels, recalled the historical significance of what Estacado was doing.

"History was being made before our very eyes, and did we know it?" Daniels asked. "No, and some of us didn't care. All we knew was a change was happening in our lives and we were going to a place that we knew nothing about. God had a plan for each and every one of us that walked through the doors of Estacado High School for the first time, and it was up to us to step into our destiny. A brand new school and a brand new plan for each of our lives; man, how awesome! No one knew what was ahead of us." Daniels continued:

> When I first heard that I was being transferred to Estacado from Dunbar, I was devastated. I felt that was the worst thing that could ever happen. I didn't care and was not concerned about integration. All I was concerned about was leaving a school that I loved and leaving my teachers, friends, and a sibling at Dunbar. I am not sure why Mom and Dad chose to send me to Estacado, but I had to go and I'm glad I did.
>
> A new environment, new teachers, new friends, and new ideas awaited us. The transition was made a little easier because some of the teachers from Dunbar went over to Estacado as well. It was great to see familiar faces within the teaching staff. Mr. Proudme, Mr. Teague, Mr. George, Mr. Jones, Mrs. Sheffield, and Mrs. Carter, just to name a few.

Estacado was a school of a new beginning, and it was up to each individual to decide and to determine what part they wanted to play, according to Moore Daniels. "For me, since I had to be there, I decided to be a part of the positive and not the negative," she stated. "I'm sure there were issues and problems because of the different races and cultures that were involved, but as a whole I think we got along very well. The many activities that were being established, and the many organizations being formed, kept many of us focused. There was a lot of work to be done to get this school rolling. For me, it was an honor to be part of this process, to be chosen to serve, and to be recognized in so many ways as

Ms. Estacado, Homecoming Queen and the drum major of our
fabulous band led by Mr. Lindsay." She continued:

> The spirit at Estacado was so high, it was hard to focus on the
> negative, and it all began with the Mighty Matadors football
> team. My God, it was absolutely unbelievable. Those guys on
> that football team took us through some high-spirited times,
> and I am so glad I was able to contribute to the spirit in a
> small way. As drum major of the band, to lead the band out
> on the field at halftime after those guys had performed so well
> gave me and the band a sense of pride. No matter what wrong
> notes may have been played or if someone was out of step,
> it was our time to show that we were proud to be Matadors.
> Making every game and cheering for every play was so excit-
> ing. I will never forget those great moments. Being selected as
> Homecoming Queen at that time gave me a sense of pride in
> knowing that I was representing one of the best high schools
> and posing for the best football team in the state.

Back on the field, Estacado was still hitting all the right notes.
The Matadors struck for two final TDs in a four-minute stretch
of the fourth quarter. First, it was Mosley's fifty-two-yard scoring bomb from reserve quarterback Daniel Johnson with 9:58
remaining. Four minutes later, Lethridge went to his right on a
sweep and cut back across the grain. Miller put the foot to both
PATs and it ended at 42–0.

"During that homecoming game against Colorado City, Coach
had me in some on defense at defensive tackle," fullback Frank
Judie points out. "They had this really fast running back [Steak-
ley], who was very quick to the line. Once, I had my head down
at the snap count, and he zipped right past me. Generally, if a
fast back gets through your defensive line that quickly, unhin-
dered and with a head of steam, he will make a big gain if not go
all the way. Our defensive backs reacted quickly, and they are just

as fast. Mike McLin, Joe Benson, and James Lester were all over him before he got ten to fifteen yards downfield."

"Moving up to the new AAA district [Colorado City had been in Class AA previously] was tough," Colorado City's Steakley said. "I do remember spraining my ankle the second or third game of the season. I actually drove to Austin to have Frank Medina [the University of Texas athletic trainer who had worked with two different Olympic teams and was nationally regarded as one of the best trainers in the world] tape my ankle on Thursday before the Snyder game. Obviously, I was not 100 percent but at least I could run on it. We also had a Colorado City doctor stick a needle in there and deaden it before the game. Of course, that wore off in the third quarter, and I finally had to take the bench. However, I kept Frank Medina's ankle tape job on for another week."

Steakley rushed for 1,030 yards in 1968 after earning all-state honors in Class AA a year earlier with 1,420 yards rushing on 238 carries. But having to travel to Austin just to get an ankle taped properly pointed out another advantage that Estacado had— its own athletic trainer E. G. Nunez, who came to Lubbock from Texas A&M. Athletic trainers at Texas high schools were still a rarity in 1968.

"Coach Nunez was ahead of his time," defensive line coach Wayne Garner said. "He gave the Estacado players expert treatment and kept them playing. We were extremely blessed to have our own trainer at Estacado. I remember that Coach Nunez had a good sense of humor and smiled frequently when he was around the coaches. But when he was around the players, he was all business because he didn't want a bunch of nonsense going on in the training room."

Estacado center Joe Rose noted having Nunez "in our school with a training room beside our dressing room, being there for all practices and two-a-days, being with the team on the road at every game. How big was that?"

Rose said the assistant trainers would precut many twelve- to eighteen-inch strips of white athletic tape and set them side by side along the edge of the training table.

"Taking the precut strips, Nunez would place one end on the outside edge of the left heel below the outer ankle, come up around the back of the foot to a spot on the lower leg high above the inside ankle in an 'S-like' pattern," Rose recalled. "Then in succession he would proceed to put on one after another of the same pattern next to, but slightly overlapping the last. Soon you had an ankle cast. It was very elaborate, but Nunez was so efficient he'd do it very quickly. Never smiled or joked when at work on his athletes. It was serious business, taping his players for the battle to come."

"I wish he had lived long enough to follow and experience the recognition given to the 1968 Matadors," E. G. Nunez's widow Melba Nunez Haulotte said. "Little did we know those guys would be making history. I believe his years with the Matadors and the coaches were the happiest of his life. The 1968 Matadors were and are an amazing group of humans."

Nunez Haulotte listed several things that made Nunez the man and the beloved athletic trainer:

Always gave 100 percent to anything he did.

Gave and expected respect from the players.

Gave directives regarding training and rehab that were to be followed implicitly.

There was a time to work and a time to kid around, and the two were not to be mixed.

Cared deeply for the players.

His goal? To win, win, win. He was highly competitive.

His mission? To keep the players healthy and ready to play by applying strength training, ongoing rehabilitation, and his well-known taping method.

With the win over Colorado City, Estacado was now 9–0 and had given up only two touchdowns all season, but in reality, the Matadors had accomplished nothing. They still needed a win against powerful Sweetwater in the regular-season finale to claim a district championship and a trip to the playoffs that came with it.

Wallace said everyone Estacado played would change up what they normally did on defense to try to stop the Matadors. "They would get in an eight- or nine-man front," he said. "The next play they would go to a 4–3 or 5–2 regular defense. We weren't smart enough to audible. Those things didn't exist the way they do today."

Chapter 10

For All the Marbles

The Associated Press had Estacado ranked No. 4 and Sweetwater No. 10 in the state in Class AAA going into the much-anticipated regular-season finale matchup between the Matadors and Mustangs. A full house of more than 8,000 attended the game at the Mustang Bowl in Sweetwater. Estacado was 9–0 and Sweetwater 7–0–1 with a game remaining against Brownfield on its schedule.

In his midweek preview of the showdown, Billy Ahrens of the *Lubbock Avalanche-Journal* noted that only one game separates Estacado from a perfect 10–0 District 3-AAA record. "That one game is with Sweetwater," he wrote. "That one game could cause more trouble than a gin-sipping mother-in-law who's decided to move in with you."

The flu bug bit the Estacado team early in the week, hitting Jesse Lethridge, Kenneth Wallace, and David Moody the hardest. But everyone was back to practice by Thursday.

The Matadors still remember the game as the hardest-hitting contest in which they had ever been involved.

Ahrens also noted the fierceness of the battle in his postgame story: "The name of the game was defense—and when all the cracking was finished, Estacado had won its tenth straight District 3-AAA battle 7–0 Friday night over the Sweetwater Mustangs at the Mustang Bowl," he wrote. The story continued:

After a scoreless first half, James Mosley scored the game's only touchdown on a six-yard struggle over left tackle with 6:02 remaining in the third quarter. Larry Miller booted the extra point. It put the game away. And it put the championship in the sack for the state's fourth-ranked AAA aggregation. After the lone touchdown, the rest of the game saw people hitting each other and creating unthinkable catastrophes.

"Sweetwater was extremely fired up," Estacado coach Jimmie Keeling told Ahrens above the shouts of his charges in a steamy dressing room. "They kept us in the hole in the first half. We tried to control the ball and clock in the second half."

Sweetwater's Mustang Bowl is one of the most famous high school football stadiums in Texas, a bowl-shaped stadium that sits below ground level and requires the opposing team to enter and exit the stadium up the stairs through the raucous home crowd.

"At halftime before leaving the field, Coach Keeling called the team together and said, 'Put your helmets on and keep them on,'" backup quarterback Daniel Johnson stated. "We had been called a lot of names before, some of them not so nice, but some of the names we heard that night were new to us. We had never before heard such words. As we went to and from the field house at halftime, all types of liquids were thrown at us. Coach Keeling kept us all as calm as he could and said, 'If they don't score, they can't beat us.'"

The Mustangs' defense, led by 200-pound tackle Randy Baker, held Estacado's steam-rolling offense to only nineteen yards rushing and twenty yards through the airways in the opening half. Sweetwater gained fifty-five yards on the ground while picking up one yard in the air during the first half.

Two short Estacado punts put Sweetwater in an advantageous field position. But each time Estacado's defense held, and Wes Ronemus failed on field goal attempts of thirty-seven and forty-six yards.

"I had not had to punt many times in the previous games and never punted under any pressure," Tommy Scruggs recalled. "That was about to change. I don't think we ever put together a series of downs that produced a first down in the first half. I had to punt every time we got the ball, and I was kicking it nearly straight up. If I got a good bounce, it might have been a fifteen-yard kick."

Estacado actually did manage two first downs in the first half but came back with five more in the second half. One was on Mosley's six-yard scoring run. Sweetwater had just six first downs against the Matadors' defense.

When the Matadors had to punt again in the third quarter, Fred White said, "Scruggs, what is wrong with you? Kick the damn ball down the field and not straight up."

"I told him if you guys will keep them off me, I will," Scruggs responded. "We took our positions, and Joe [Rose] snapped the ball. All of Sweetwater's team had moved up, expecting a kick like the last ten kicks. Fred and the rest of the team gave me enough time, and somehow instead of the ball going straight up, it went downfield and over the heads of the Sweetwater guys. Fred said, 'Good job, Scruggs.' I thought how lucky can a guy get? We won that game, and that was when I began to realize we had something really special. Coach had kept us motivated, moving in the same direction. We were still all together, and it felt good. I was beginning to feel comfortable playing ball with these guys."

That third-quarter punt was a booming fifty-seven-yarder by Scruggs, pinning Sweetwater back on its eight-yard line. It couldn't move against a defense led by linebacker White, cornerbacks Mike McLin and David Moody, and safety Joe Benson.

The Mustangs punted and Estacado went to work on the Sweetwater forty-three. So did Mosley. The 210-pound tailback moved the ball to the thirty in three carries. Then quarterback

Kenneth Wallace rolled around left end and found daylight. He rambled to the Sweetwater twelve before he was stopped.

A personal foul moved the ball to the six. And from there, Ahrens wrote, "you know the rest of story."

"That was the toughest game we had all year," Mosley said of the Sweetwater victory. "It was back and forth in the middle of the field pretty much the whole night. If they would have won, I think they would have won the state championship because they were just that good. We got a break and moved the ball down the field. Our line did just enough to help me get into the end zone. It was an off-tackle play run to the left side. I didn't have the speed to get outside, so I took the quickest route."

Wingback Larry Miller was Estacado's leading rusher with forty-five yards on seventeen carries. Mosley picked up thirty-eight yards on sixteen attempts. Fullback Benjie Kemp, who had Sweetwater's longest run of twenty-one yards, finished the night with fifty yards on twelve carries.

Sweetwater's deepest penetration came on its first offensive series and reached the Estacado nineteen-yard line. Except for the one Matador score, Estacado could reach only the Sweetwater twenty-three.

The next day following the hard-hitting contest, many of the Estacado players admitted in the Lubbock paper that they were sore.

"I'm plenty sore today," Miller stated.

"My hands are sore," added Mosley.

"My ribs and chest are hurting today," commented Wallace. "I knew it was going to be hard, but I thought we would win by more. I think we are going to have to play better."

Safety Joe Benson, who saved a touchdown when he hauled down Sweetwater's Aubrey McCain after a long gainer, said winning district didn't surprise him. "We had our goal set for state, so we had to win all ten," Benson told Ahrens, praising his defensive teammates for stopping Kemp, the Mustangs' talented running back. "Fred White [middle linebacker] and Freddie Stephens [tackle] stopped up the middle and the outside."

Not only did Estacado finish the regular season with a 10–0 mark, the Matadors also outscored their opponents 431–12, a testament to the team's outstanding defense. And now, the Estacado players could turn their attention to the playoffs and the final four rungs to complete their ladder.

Chapter 11

Slaying the Lions

Following the knock-down, drag-out win over Sweetwater, the Matadors had a week off as the rest of the District 3-AAA teams wrapped up the regular season with nothing to play for. Estacado already had the district championship secured. But the Matadors had to wait to find out who their bi-district opponent would be in the first round of the playoffs.

The answer was Brownwood, the defending state champion and perhaps the most feared Class AAA team in the state. The Lions, who returned nine lettermen but just two starters from their 1967 team that had finished 12–1–1 en route to winning the state title, were led by coach Gordon Wood, who had already won two state championships at Stamford (Lubbock Independent School District athletic director Pete Ragus had been on Wood's staff at Stamford in the 1950s) and three more at Brownwood since taking over the Lions' program in 1960. He would end his career as the nation's winningest high school football coach. Before Wood was finished, he would claim four more state titles in a twenty-five-year career at Brownwood.

Not in 1968, however. The Matadors handed Wood his worst loss, pounding the Lions 49–8 in a Thanksgiving Day game in Abilene.

The rest of Lubbock was starting to pay attention to the 10–0 Matadors. Lubbock mayor W. D. "Dub" Rogers and Texas Tech coach J. T. King attended Estacado's pep rally the day before the game, and Rogers presented a city council proclamation making Thanksgiving Day "Estacado Matador Day."

"I wanted to see what it was like to rub shoulders with a winner," King told the gathering at the pep rally.

The Dunbar cheerleaders also attended the pep rally, declaring their support for the rival Matadors.

The Estacado support groups were getting involved in the excitement of the playoffs, too. "When the team made the playoffs, we wanted to do more to show our support," said Melinda Mims Hedgcoth. "A few cheerleaders and I made signs with words to yell and slogans for that week on them. We attached a piece of wood to the signs so we could stick them in the ground. We left really early and put the signs out on the road to the game. I really think the team liked them, and we liked making them. We wanted to 'fire' them up! Bobby Lester, one of the players, came up with our fight song 'STOP, LOOK and LISTEN,' and we sang it at pep rallies, games, and everywhere we could."

What road the Matadors would take to that first playoff game against Brownwood, however, turned out to be an interesting story.

"We wanted to play on Thursday [Thanksgiving Day] because we knew it was an advantage since our last playing date was open," Estacado coach Jimmie Keeling said. "Gordon wanted to play in Abilene. We held out for Sweetwater since I knew he didn't want to play there because they had lost a playoff game against Dumas in Sweetwater a year or so before. We even agreed to play on Saturday in Sweetwater since I knew he would not do it. We were just trying to gain leverage to play on Thanksgiving Day. He loved playing at Shotwell Stadium in Abilene. We agreed to play at Shotwell if we played on Thursday, which was Thanksgiving. Gordon actually liked playing on Thanksgiving afternoon and had played several playoff games before on Thanksgiving. Just a cat-and-mouse game between good friends that both wanted to win badly."

Wood, however, shared a slightly different memory in an article he wrote for the *Brownwood Bulletin* later, following the lopsided loss to Estacado. "I read where a psychiatrist, studying the results of an emotional game, said that players could not fully recover from a big game in less than eight days," Wood wrote. "He said they could partially recover in seven days, but six or five days would be extremely harmful to their performance. The Matadors had the week off before our game and had spent the week preparing for Wichita Falls Washington or the Brownwood Lions." The article continued:

> When we met with Jimmie Keeling, the Estacado coach, he held out for a Thursday game, knowing full well this would give him a great edge over us and because they were already prepared to play and we would only have three days to prepare for them. Also, this would give them an advantage for their next opponent, if they won. We flipped a coin with the game to be either on Thursday or Saturday. We missed the call, and the game was set for Thursday at Shotwell Stadium.

Part of the story of the win over Brownwood is what happened before the game. It had snowed earlier in the week, and then it warmed up and much of the snow melted, leaving Abilene's Shotwell Stadium a muddy mess.

"There was snow still on the turf," quarterback Kenneth Wallace recalled. "When we were in the locker room, Hollis Gainey and the other coaches were shoveling snow off the field."

"Coach Gainey cleaned the field off himself," running back James Mosley added. "Because I had a low center of gravity, it worked well for me. Everyone else was slipping. I like running in the mud."

Keeling said he called Bill Kelly with the athletic supply store in Lubbock the night before the game and acquired some longer cleats, which the coaches put on the players' shoes, making them better equipped to handle the muddy conditions.

"Coach Keeling had everyone change their cleats to two-inch, two-and-a-half-inch or three-inch cleats," said backup quarterback Daniel Johnson. "That was a great, great move. James Lester and Jesse Lethridge were like jackrabbits running the ball. James Mosley, Larry Miller, and Frank Judie, our power backs, did their thing."

Not only did the team put longer cleats on their shoes, Wallace said he also taped tacks on his hand. "I tried that, but the tacks had to go," he said. "I said, 'No, Coach, I can't do that.'"

"We felt we could prepare well, physically, in five days, but we were not prepared for what happened," Wood wrote in the Brownwood newspaper. "The week of our game, we had freezing weather, rain, sleet, and snow on Monday, Tuesday, and Wednesday. We were unable to get any work done and were not prepared to play, mentally." Wood continued:

> On Thursday, we arrived at Abilene and Coach Keeling had taken his team and with the help of the Abilene schools, they had rolled the snow off the field, but left considerable sleet and ice on the field.
>
> At midnight before the Thursday game, Coach Keeling got a sporting goods salesman out of bed, and they opened up their store and searched it and found old-time mud cleats that were twice as long and sharp as the modern cleats. I never used mud cleats because they cause mud to be thicker on the shoes. Jimmie tested these shoes and his regular shoes and found that they cut through the sleet, and the footing was much better than the normal cleats, and the footing was good. Their backs could cut and drive, and ours would cut and slip. This game was a total mismatch.

Even Wood admitted, however, that "Estacado would have beaten us anyway because of the other aspects of the game. Estacado had a great team and great coaching. They won the state championship easily."

Despite the slippery conditions, Wallace said he hit Freddie Stephens on a sixty-yard bootleg pass on the game's first play. "We never looked back after that," Wallace claimed.

Billy Ahrens had a great line in his game story in the *Lubbock Avalanche-Journal*: "It was the worst whipping Brownwood coach Gordon Wood had received since his daddy took a strap to him when he was twelve years old," Ahrens quipped. "Wood, a mild-mannered coach who is better known for building schoolboy state champions, watched Estacado do unhuman things to his charges Thursday at P. E. Shotwell Stadium in Abilene." He wrote:

> When Estacado had finished its thing, 49–8, Wood dropped his head, kicked at the muddy turf and walked to the middle of the field to shake Jimmie Keeling's hand. It was the worst whipping a Wood-coached Brownwood team had ever received. That's since 1960, the first of three times Brownwood rolled to the AAA state title. Before this, it was a 43–13 setback at the hands of quarterback Jack Mildren and AAAA state runner-up Abilene Cooper the past year.
>
> Estacado, behind the running of Larry Miller who scored three TDs, scored twenty-one points in the third period and had a defense that wouldn't stop. It finished off the defending state champs. The Matadors intercepted four Brownwood passes and recovered four fumbles.

Two days after the Matadors' dismantling of Brownwood, Wood was still raving about Estacado's performance against his Lions. "If Estacado doesn't win state," said Wood, "I'd hate to play the team that does." Wood's comments came in Ahrens's Sunday column "Rolling Down Playoff Lane."

Jimmy Carmichael, who was a sophomore on Brownwood's 1967 state championship team that defeated Dunbar 28–0 in Dunbar's first season as a UIL team, was the starting quarterback for the Lions in the 1968 loss to Estacado. A year later, he was the quarterback when Brownwood exacted revenge and beat the Matadors, handing Estacado its first varsity loss in two years, en route to claiming Brownwood's second state title in three years. He called the 1968 game "the worst loss that I ever experienced."

"I have told this story hundreds of times over my life," Carmichael said. "The fact that a brand new first-class team could run the tables and win it all was more than amazing. The Estacado team had a unique combination of great talent and a great coach. I have been a fan of Jimmie Keeling for a long time. And I have told him so on many occasions. He is a class act, and a damn fine coach. The 1968 game, combined with the following 1969 game, represents one of the greatest stories in Texas high school football. I was fortunate to be humbled in the 1968 game, and more fortunate to be able to find a measure of redemption in the 1969 game. Many of the Estacado players became teammates [at Texas Tech]—James Mosley, Kenneth Wallace, and Larry Miller—and friends of mine. All are very good guys, and I am proud to call them my friends."

Ahrens, who noted the Matadors' next opponent would be Kermit, also joked, "Keeling, who is more pessimistic than a hypochondriac on his death bed, says, 'I feel like this is a real key game for us. Kermit has got overall better athletes than we've faced this year. They have 22 seniors, which always helps.'"

Ahrens also wrote, "Kermit is tougher than raw steak."

Chapter 12

Surviving an Air Attack

While the Estacado football team was continuing its playoff run, race relations and the changing world was never far from the public eye in Lubbock. President Lyndon Johnson signed the Civil Rights Act in 1968, and a ruling of the US Supreme Court that year said all housing would have to be open and available to all races.

Even the *Estacado Echo*, the school newspaper, carried a story on November 25 about a citizens' group's plan to "rebuild" northeast Lubbock. "A plan has recently been undertaken by citizens of northeast Lubbock to make the community a better place for all races to live," the *Echo* wrote. "It is a plan that will let different races live together and work together in an All American Community." The article continued:

> The citizens plan to make the area north of Parkway Drive, immediately east of McKenzie Park and just inside Loop 289, a better community and a showcase of integration to all American cities.
>
> In 1962 and 1963, this area began to develop and was thought to be one of the most desirable areas of Lubbock for several reasons. The prospects for total development looked promising, and then something happened. Housing in the $10,000 to $15,000 cost range has been over-built, causing abandonment

of contracts, foreclosure by lending agencies and repossession by FHA.

Families from the Negro community began to buy in this area and reaction of the white population was typical and expected. With the movement in of the Negro population came the moving out of the white. To make matters worse, some of the new families had over-indebted themselves and were unable to retain the houses, thus began moving out, causing even more vacancies.

Distrust and lack of understanding between races only served to reinforce the deterioration of the community while vandalism, wrecking of unoccupied houses and theft apparently sealed the doom.

The story said the purpose of the plan was to not only help the community and its residents but to also help overcome distrust between all races.

In an editorial in the same issue of the *Estacado Echo*, the school newspaper wrote, "Can a community that rose from a cotton field to a vibrant area of middle class homes and then dipped into a definite slump, come back from the dead and become a bustling community again? On one block alone, thirty-one houses stand vacant, and uncounted numbers stand vacant on other blocks. Many have been ripped and torn apart by vandalism and theft." The editorial continued:

> All of this has happened because of racial distrust and lack of respect for the law and other people. In the words of realtor, Mr. Joe B. Phillips, "Right now, Northeast Lubbock is a black eye to the city. We hope to make it something of which to be proud."
>
> The question is, "Can we, as a unified group of citizens, change this blackened area into something we can be proud of?" It's not going to be easy, and it's going to take everyone in the community to get something done. Can we? We can and we must.

Mark Bass, a financial adviser in Lubbock whose father, Roy Bass, was mayor of Lubbock from 1974 to 1978, was a senior at Lubbock Monterey in 1968. He remembered thinking "it was cool for them and cool for Lubbock" that the Estacado football team was having success.

"As you know, 1968 was a momentous year," Bass said. "In the wake of the assassinations of Robert Kennedy and Martin Luther King Jr., one of the ministers at our church, Second Baptist, Robert Wells, reached out and developed a discussion group for some kids from our church [all white] and kids from another church on the east side of Lubbock [all black]. I don't recall exactly, but we met every couple of weeks for the better part of a year or more to discuss current events in the US and how we could improve race relations in Lubbock. I don't remember how many kids were involved, maybe ten or twenty, but if nothing else, it gave all of those involved a better understanding of each other. It seemed at the time that we were improving race relations in our own small way, even if it was just with each other in that group."

Although white flight and distrust between the races was obviously a problem in Lubbock in 1968, there was one thing that all races could understand—a winning football team. As the Matadors continued their winning streak, more and more people, including politicians, were jumping on the Estacado bandwagon. Kermit was the next opponent, and governor-elect Preston Smith was the guest speaker for the pep rally. He was joined on the stage by LISD athletic director Pete Ragus, as well as the Lubbock Monterey cheerleaders who represented the support of their school.

Kermit, which returned twenty-two seniors from a 9–1 team in 1967, presented a new challenge for Estacado in the Matadors' quarterfinal playoff game. The Yellow Jackets' quarterback Tim Peden threw for 2,020 yards in 1968 and 4,410 career yards in his two years as Kermit's starting quarterback. But once again, the Estacado defense was up for the challenge.

"It's a good thing Estacado doesn't get air sick," Billy Ahrens wrote in the *Lubbock Avalanche-Journal.* "That's where the football was most of the time in Kermit Saturday afternoon. Kermit quarterback Tim Peden pitched for 319 yards through the airways. But it didn't mean a thing." Ahrens continued:

> Estacado, sticking with its steamrolling ground game, overcame Peden, an out-of-town crowd of 7,000 and the Kermit police to rip the Yellow Jackets 35–12 and advance into the semifinals of the Class AAA schoolboy playoffs.
>
> Kermit didn't do so well on the ground. Estacado's hardnosed defense, led by Fred White and a host of others, held Kermit to four yards rushing, but the twelve points were the most scored on the Matadors as the first-year UIL member rolled up its twelfth straight victory. The Matador defense dropped Peden five times for thirty-seven yards in losses.

Larry Miller led Estacado with seventy-nine yards and two touchdowns rushing on eleven carries. Quarterback Kenneth Wallace added seventy-one yards and two more scores on eight attempts, although the junior signal caller suffered an ankle injury in the final period.

Jesse Lethridge and James Mosley scored the other two touchdowns, and Miller booted five extra points.

"The final minutes of the game saw two minor fights," Ahrens wrote. "The first one saw a couple of Kermit policemen step into the melee. It was soon cleared up, and no one yelled about brutality."

"There was a lot of uneasiness in the Kermit game," Estacado coach Jimmie Keeling said. "We were ready to whip tail and get out of there."

The six two, 195-pound Peden used the short passing game to rack up the yardage against Estacado. Mike Hodges snagged thirteen catches for 171 yards, while Howard Porter pulled in seven receptions for ninety-four yards.

But Estacado's 327 yards on the ground sacked up the quarterfinals battle.

The opening half was reminiscent of the previous week's Brownwood battle. Estacado scored once in the first period and three times in the second. The only difference was Kermit also scored.

"A 28–6 lead looked as though it would be hard to overcome and droves of Kermit fans split for the casa and warmth," Ahrens wrote.

Estacado's first score came eight minutes deep into the first quarter. Estacado started at its twenty and soon moved to the Kermit nineteen on runs by Mosley, Frank Judie, and Miller. From the nineteen, Wallace rolled to his right and strutted into the end zone.

On the Matadors' first series in the second stanza, another seven points seemed certain to come. Safety Joe Benson intercepted his fifth pass of the year at his forty-three and returned to the Kermit forty-seven-yard line. Six plays later, with 9:10 remaining, Miller blasted over left tackle and converted to stretch Estacado's lead to 14–0.

An interception by White set up another quick Estacado score to make it 21–0.

A sign hanging on the Matadors' side of the field was getting easier to believe. It read "Matadors Say State in '68 Would Be Great."

Chapter 13

A Smothering Defense

One step remained on the ladder in the Estacado locker room for the Matadors to reach the Class AAA state title game. And it wouldn't be easy, as Estacado, the best team in West Texas, had to face Henderson, the best team from East Texas.

The Lions were led by two-time all-state running back Joe Wylie, who went on to earn all-Big-Eight honors at the University of Oklahoma and be inducted into the Texas High School Football Hall of Fame. Wylie had rushed for nearly 2,000 yards and thirty-four touchdowns, and he was being compared to Palestine's Bill Bradley as the best do-it-all athlete to come out of East Texas at the time. Wylie finished his high school career with sixty-four touchdowns, and at Oklahoma he was a starting halfback on the most prolific rushing attack in college football history. The Sooners averaged 472.4 yards rushing per game in 1971. Wylie finished his collegiate career with 1,653 yards rushing and twenty touchdowns, playing in a backfield with all-Americans Jack Mildren from Abilene Cooper and Greg Pruitt. His 28.5 yards per kickoff return stood as a collegiate record for twenty-seven years.

KLBK sports broadcaster Sammy Smith and Lubbock High student body president Arthur Fletcher were the guest speakers at the Matadors' pep rally. Smith spent much of his speech waxing praise on Wylie and warning the Estacado defense. Henderson was riding an eighteen-game winning streak.

Despite his lofty past and future statistics, Wylie could do little against the stingy Matadors. The state semifinal game was set for Abilene's Shotwell Stadium, the same site where the Matadors had walloped Coach Gordon Wood's Brownwood Lions in their bi-district contest. The result was much the same, as Wylie and Henderson were no match for Estacado's smothering defense. The Matadors mauled Henderson 30–0 to capture their thirteenth consecutive victory.

Wylie had rushed for 1,940 yards through the first twelve games of the season, but he could muster only ninety-two yards on twenty-five carries against the Matadors, and the majority of those yards came in the closing minutes of the game. The Estacado defense sacked quarterback Keith Bobo ten times for a minus thirty-nine yards.

"That game stands out," Estacado defensive line coach Wayne Garner recalled. "Henderson had a great running back in Joe Wylie, and we were able to shut him down. Our team speed on defense was incredible, and [linebacker] Fred White's ability to run from sideline to sideline was amazing."

Quarterback Kenneth Wallace, who had been injured several weeks earlier, led the Matadors to a 16–0 halftime lead. Estacado gained 204 yards rushing compared to the Lions' 110, and Wallace also threw a touchdown pass.

James Mosley, who finished with fifty-four yards on thirteen carries, tallied the first score of the game on a three-yard run. A thirty-five-yard punt return by Marvin Turner set up Larry Miller's twenty-nine-yard field goal, his first three-pointer of the season. Linebacker Fred White intercepted a halfback pass thrown by Wylie in the second quarter, putting the Matadors in position to increase their lead to 16–0 on Ronnie Hill's twenty-three-yard TD reception from Wallace.

A fumble recovery gave Henderson its best scoring opportunity late in the second quarter. Henderson advanced to the Estacado five-yard line, but White and Walter Hibbler sacked Bobo at the twenty-one-yard line.

In the fourth quarter, James Lester returned a punt seventy-six yards for a touchdown, and then reserve quarterback Daniel Johnson scored the final touchdown on a five-yard run with one minute left in the game.

Wallace said he watched the Matadors' defense totally shut down Wylie. "Willie Avery was on our practice squad," Wallace said. "He was Joe Wylie in practice before the Henderson game and A. G. Perryman before the Dunbar game. Our defense would light him up. He deserves part of the state championship trophy."

"For the record, in that 1968 season, there was one team that scored on the Mighty Matador defense every week, scored more points against them than all their other opponents combined that season," Estacado backup Jesse Bozeman emphasized. "Daniel Johnson or myself would quarterback the practice squad offense each week against the first-time defense. Coach Keeling actually ran the scout team offense. He'd say, 'run it again, run it again, I want to make sure they know it's coming!'" Bozeman continued:

> Willie Avery, Avance Green, Joe Benson, Porter Jaushlin, and Marvin Turner were alternating backs, depending on the style of the opponent's backfield. We had a good offensive line, too. Yes, we got beat up pretty bad, but we would score on them every week. So, someone needs to make sure that these guys get recognition because I don't think we would have won all those games without the contributions by this unit and these guys.

Wylie said Henderson had only two black players on the 1968 varsity team, one senior and one junior. "Thinking back now, Henderson Hill High [that community's black high school] had a good football team, and I bet their coaches didn't want to give up any of their top talent at the beginning of integration," contemplated Wylie. "Three years later, Joe Paul Paige was the Henderson tailback, and he went to Baylor on scholarship. I bet there were some guys over at Hill High in 1968 that could have really helped us."

Nearly fifty years later, Wylie, who is now a certified public accountant in Tyler, is amazed with what Estacado accomplished. "Against a backdrop of unrest in our country, a group of young men banded together and accomplished a feat unique in Texas high school football lore, a state championship in their high school's first varsity season," he said. "This story is inspiration to all of us, how to face change with hard work and teamwork, even to those of us who gave our best to defeat the 1968 Lubbock Estacado Matadors."

Despite the big win, fullback Frank Judie was impressed by Henderson. He said every team from the regular-season finale against Sweetwater and throughout the playoffs had gotten better and were better prepared.

"Against Henderson, I remember their two defensive ends being like bookends," he recalled. "Both were about six-foot-one and 190 or 200 pounds. On a typical tailback-left play, I would kick out to take on their right defensive end. I'm focused on planting my helmet in his middle chest and driving him out of the play. I saw the defensive end remaining in a crouch with his left hand extended and his right arm hanging down. He used that hand to push my helmet and stand me up for that right arm to swing up and into my crotch. It surprised me, and I will admit it hurt a bit. A few plays later, we were running tailback-right, and I was heading for their left defensive end. He took the same crouch with one arm extended and one hanging down. Same technique, pushed my helmet and swung the other arm into my crotch. Sometimes it was effective, other times not. But it was the same the whole game. It was perfectly legal, and they had obviously practiced it to have some effect on our tailback's lead blocker."

What might have seemed improbable just a few months earlier was becoming a reality. The Estacado team, which had never lost a varsity game in its one and only season and just one game as a junior varsity a year earlier against larger District 4-AAAA schools, was headed to the state championship game, a 2:00 p.m. matchup the following Saturday at Texas Christian University's Amon Carter Stadium in Fort Worth against perennial South Texas powerhouse Refugio.

Wallace recalled after the Matadors' last hard practice before heading to Fort Worth to face Refugio that he asked Coach Jimmie Keeling, "Coach, be honest. Is this team any good? He couldn't have given me a better answer. He said, 'Kenneth, the state championship game is designed for the best two teams to meet.' We went into every game thinking that this team is good and would be the toughest opponent we would face. I figured it out. Coach Keeling said, 'Those guys are going to get after your butts.'"

With the success the Matadors were enjoying, attitudes related to the Estacado football team changed, according to Wallace. "Estacado had the whole east side of Lubbock in our hand," he said, "and eventually all of Lubbock. In public, I was shy. I didn't need publicity. My dad's boss was even talking about our football team. He had a whole different outlook. His boss would brag to other folks about our football team. Even at church, the preacher and the deacons, and even the old ladies who I thought didn't know anything about football, were all talking about Estacado football."

Still, one more rung needed to be climbed, however, to complete the Matadors' dream season.

Chapter 14

14–0

It normally takes years to build a championship program. But Estacado entered the state championship game at TCU's Amon Carter Stadium with the opportunity to do something that no other Texas high school had ever done—win a state title in its first year of varsity football.

Standing in the Matadors' way, however, was the best team from South Texas, and unbeaten Refugio had the speed to match Estacado's. Refugio had won a shoot-out 55–44 over Alvin to earn its berth in the state title game behind Eugene "Bull" Lewis's 195 yards and four touchdowns rushing. He also threw for another TD as the Bobcats compiled 470 yards total offense.

The Estacado team arrived in Fort Worth on Friday, and linebacker David Moody still laughs as he remembered the team going to a movie the night before the big game. "We went to the movie *Candy*," he chuckled. "We thought it was rated G, but it was X-rated. You couldn't get us out of the theater fast enough."

A mix-up on the movie didn't seem to impact the Matadors the following day.

The first day of winter brought a chilly, misty day in Fort Worth.

Estacado student Melinda Mims Hedgcoth remembered the start of the title game not for the weather but for another reason one might not suspect. "There was a new TV station in Lubbock, and they were following Estacado through our playoff excitement," she commented. "Glenda [Rankin] and I were holding the run-through sign at the state championship game. Some of the team thought it would be real fun to tear big pieces of the sign and carry them out to the fifty-yard line. Guess who had to pick up the pieces? Me! I bent over to pick up the pieces of paper on the field, and when I looked up, the camera from the TV station was right in my face. I was on the ten o'clock news. Ha! Of course, the game highlights were, too."

Billy Ahrens, writing in the *Lubbock Avalanche-Journal*, noted, "As the two aggregations lined up for the upcoming kickoff, twenty-two individuals were more nervous than a cat in a violin factory. Refugio proved to be the more nervous. Estacado and Refugio whipped Refugio in the opening half."

The Matadors, just as they had done all season, used a powerful running game and a tenacious defense. Estacado scored two first-quarter touchdowns and held Refugio at bay for three quarters to capture the Texas title.

Larry Miller booted the opening kickoff into the end zone, and Refugio started at its own twenty. A twenty-five-yard pass play from Lewis to Edward Daniels moved the Bobcats to the Estacado forty-nine. Next came runs by Efren Gipson and Lewis as Refugio advanced to the Matadors' twenty-yard line. But on fourth-and-thirteen from the twenty-six-yard line, Mike Davis's pass to Gipson in the end zone was blocked by linebacker David Moody, and Estacado finally had possession.

"Refugio took the opening kickoff and marched down the field with the quarterback under center," Matadors defensive line coach Wayne Garner said. "They got inside the ten-yard line and then they went to the shotgun and we threw them for an incredible loss of yardage. I never did understand why they shifted to the shotgun, but it was an outstanding defensive effort on our part."

Estacado had the ball twice in opening quarter and scored both times.

After Refugio's drive stalled at the Estacado twenty-six, the Matadors' offense went to work. Runs by Miller, James Mosley, and Frank Judie moved the ball to the Matador forty-three.

Then quarterback Kenneth Wallace hit on one of his two passes. Wallace faded back and saw end Tommy Scruggs alone at the Refugio thirty-yard line and let sail. Scruggs caught it without breaking stride and was finally overhauled at the eleven. It was just Scruggs's second reception of the season (the other came against Dunbar).

Then Mosley ran for a yard and Wallace rolled for two more. On third-and-seven from the eight-yard line, Miller broke off right tackle and made a mad dash for the end zone. But Gary Lott was there. Judie took out Lott with a block and Miller scored with 5:34 remaining. Miller then converted the extra point kick to give Estacado a 7–0 lead.

Refugio got it back, but couldn't budge, and Lewis got off a twenty-five-yard punt to the Estacado forty-nine. Eight plays later, with twenty-four ticks remaining in the first quarter, Mosley rambled eleven yards untouched and Miller converted to make it 14–0 and end the scoring.

Refugio's deepest penetration of the game came in the closing minutes of the second quarter. And it was about as deep as one could get without scoring.

Estacado's Homer Morse picked off Lewis's pass and was dropped at his five. The Matadors couldn't move and Scruggs's twenty-seven-yard punt gave the Bobcats possession at the Estacado thirty-three.

With Lewis running and passing out of a shotgun formation, Refugio drove to the seven. On the next play, Lewis ran up the gut and was stopped at the two by Mike McLin and James Lester.

Lewis then sneaked to the six-inch line for a first down. But Refugio couldn't punch it in. Ahrens described it in the next day's newspaper: "This was when Refugio beat Refugio," he wrote. "The Bobcats went back to a shotgun with Lewis at the controls.

On the first down, Lewis dug out for the goal and was stopped at the three by Robert Boykin. Then Lewis, still in the shotgun, pitched a flat pass to Gipson and again Boykin stopped it at the three, making it third-and-goal at the three. Mike Davis came back in at quarterback. He pitched to Lewis, who attempted to pass to Lott, but Miller broke it up. On fourth down, Gipson fumbled on a double reverse after Walter Hibbler shocked him, and David Moody pounced on the ball at the three as the half ended. From then on, for all practical purposes, the game was over when Refugio failed to score."

Refugio won the statistics battle, 252–245, but most of its yardage came between the twenty-yard lines. Most of its rushing and passing yardage came in the second half.

Once again, the running of Mosley and Miller finished the opposition. Both scored a touchdown and Miller booted the conversions. Linemen Scruggs, William Hall, Boykin, Joe Rose, Moody, Robert Hines, and J. B. Lemon opened holes for Miller and Mosley consistently.

Mosley, a six foot, 210-pound tailback, carried the ball nineteen times for eighty-seven yards. Miller, a six two, 189-pound wingback, rushed for fifty-five yards on fifteen assignments.

The Estacado defense led by middle linebacker Fred White, Boykin, and cornerback Marvin Turner, who intercepted two passes, held Refugio's talented running back Lewis to seventy-one yards on fifteen carries.

And when it came to making yards and razzle-dazzle, Lewis was the only thing Refugio had.

Refugio threatened in the second half. Miller misfired on a third-quarter field goal try. Refugio then advanced to the Matadors' thirty-one, but Lott's fourth-down pass to Raymond Anderson was incomplete in the end zone.

The next time the Bobcats got the ball, they made it to the fourteen-yard line, where Davis pitched back wildly and White recovered for the Matadors on the first play of the final quarter.

Another Refugio push to the thirty-one ended with Davis misfiring on a pitchout and Marvin Turner pouncing on the loose ball for Estacado.

Refugio used a trick formation to drive to the Estacado eleven-yard line in the final stages of the game. The Bobcats' entire offensive wall lined up on the right side of the field with two flankers on the left side in a formation sometimes called the swinging gate.

The Refugio center remained in the middle of the field with Lewis in shotgun formation. It almost worked, but Lewis's third-down pass was picked off by Turner, and Estacado held on to the ball for the final 1:56.

Not only was Mosley a workhorse for Estacado with eighty-seven yards rushing, including sixty-one in the first half, but he also gained nineteen yards in the first TD drive and thirty-eight in the second.

Lewis totaled seventy-one yards rushing for Refugio, which finished with a 14–1 record. Estacado completed the championship season with a spotless 14–0 mark.

"Estacado's dressing room was wilder than Kate Smith doing the monkey," Ahrens wrote, noting Estacado's state title was the first for a Lubbock team to win in UIL competition since Lubbock High turned the trick in 1952.

"It was euphoria," Mosley said of the state championship game victory. "That is what you worked for the whole year. We saw some plays from the other team [Refugio] that we had never seen before. When they got in that spread, we didn't know what to do. That game, that was what you play for."

Defensive coordinator Delbert Wilson's defensive unit gave up only thirty-two points in fourteen games in completing a 14–0 season. "It was not just that they were good football players, they were good people," he said.

There was a funny moment in the state championship game for Wilson, however. "It was a cold day, and I had an overcoat and gloves on," he recalled. "I was calling defensive signals, and one of our fans asked what are you doing giving the 'Black Power" sign? I said what are you talking about? I hadn't even thought about that."

Remember, at the Summer Olympics in Mexico City earlier that year, Tommie Smith and John Carlos, the gold and bronze medal winners in the 200-meter dash, respectively, had used the medal podium for a black fist salute.

"When we played in TCU's stadium [against Refugio in the state championship game]," defensive tackle Angel Rodriguez said, "I will never forget that."

"It was miracle how Coach Keeling melded that group together," Garner added. "Those friendships have lasted more than fifty years. It is amazing."

No doubt. But for the Mighty Matadors—and all football fans in Lubbock and throughout Texas—it was more than just winning a state championship. It was a remarkable historic journey by a unique group of athletes that bonded to lead Estacado to the state championship victory and prove that athletes and students of all races could come together to be friends and teammates.

"Usually it takes years to build a sound high school football program," Ahrens wrote in his postgame column. "It takes even longer to win the state championship. Some fifteen weeks ago, numerous Class AAA teams began two-a-day workouts in hopes of reaching the state finals." Ahrens continued:

> Estacado, in its second year of existence, was one of the many as it was embarking on its first year in the University Interscholastic League. Estacado coach Jimmie Keeling was hit by one disaster after another as the first District 3-AAA contest drew near. People quit. Others moved away.
>
> But the champions, as Keeling always called them, stuck with it. Saturday, after fourteen straight victories, the season ended in Fort Worth on a chilly, fog-shrouded day before some 7,000.

Members of the 1968 Estacado football team weren't black or brown or white. They were blue and silver Matadors. Color them champions, one of the most remarkable teams in Texas history to win a state title.

Epilogue

Changing Lives

It has been nearly fifty years since that group of Lubbock Estacado Matadors not only defied all odds by winning a state championship in the school's first season of varsity football but also proved to many doubters that players of different races could become closely bonded teammates and find success as a team.

Not only did they find success on the gridiron, but many have also enjoyed great success—and friendship—in their lives in the nearly fifty years that have followed.

Several players on that 1968 Estacado team—black linebacker David Moody, black lineman Walter Hibbler, black linebacker Fred White, white tight end Tommy Scruggs, white center Joe Rose, and black quarterback Kenneth Wallace—and coach Jimmie Keeling put together their personal reflections on how their lives were changed by the circumstances surrounding the Estacado Matadors.

Moody, who has spent the last forty-one years coaching after graduating from Estacado, earned all-state honors in 1970. He played collegiate football at West Texas State, leading the Buffaloes to a Missouri Valley Conference co-championship in 1972. After graduation from West Texas State in 1974, he entered private business before going into coaching at Lamar Consolidated

(1977–79) and San Angelo Central (1980–84) with Keeling. His coaching career included five seasons at Angelo State and four years at Rice University before joining Spike Dykes's staff at Texas Tech as a receivers coach. While at Texas Tech, Moody interned with the Buffalo Bills in 1997 and the Miami Dolphins in 1998.

When Dykes retired following the 1999 season, Moody spent one season at Lubbock Coronado before accepting the job in 2001 as the fourth head coach in Estacado history, enabling him to coach at his alma mater. In 2003, Moody resigned at Estacado and has spent the last twelve years as the assistant head coach and defensive line coach at Lubbock High School.

He and his wife have two daughters D'Metrice and LaShaunda, and a son, David III, who is an assistant principal at Lubbock Estacado.

I was the first in my family to graduate from high school and go to college. I can remember every day after practice Coach Keeling would ask us what we were going to be doing with our lives ten years from now. Most didn't know what we were going to be doing with our lives at all. He gave us a dream and most of all—hope.

Lubbock was extremely segregated. The community I lived in was a very low socio-economic community. Our country was in the middle of a civil rights movement. There was a lot of hatred between blacks and whites in Lubbock. I was told my whole life that black people and white people could not get along, and you could not trust whites.

My mom had a third-grade education and my dad never went to school because he had to work to help support his family.

We lived in a one-bedroom house with no running water. When we used the restroom, we had to use an outdoor toilet. Growing up in East Lubbock, my early childhood and my elementary school years were totally segregated. I went to Phyllis Wheatley Elementary School and Martin Elementary. I started to notice there were other races when I was in middle school, as we had Hispanics and whites.

This is really hard to talk about, and middle school was a tough adjustment. I could see the difference economically, socially, and educationally. I will never forget a great, amazing teacher that I had at this time. Her name was Mrs. Rowlett. She told me that I was a good student, but that I could be a great student if I worked hard. This was the first time I remember a teacher telling me that I could be a good student. My life slowly started to change academically.

My ninth-grade year things really started to change when I met a coach, who I thought was a probation officer when I first saw him. At this point, my life truly changed forever.

In January of 1967, Lubbock Estacado hired its first head football coach. The school opened in the fall of 1967, and the new head football coach was Jimmie Keeling. I had no idea that he would change our community, my life and so many other players' lives forever. Jimmie Keeling was more than a football coach. He became a Dad and Father figure for so many Matadors.

Coach Keeling gave me my first job when I graduated from college. The most amazing thing is that I had never been around very many white people, and he was the first white man I put my faith and trust in.

Coach Keeling came into this environment and created trust and faith and belief in each other—and amazing things happened!

The very first year we played a junior varsity schedule, and our record was nine wins and one loss. In 1968, our second year as a school and football program, we won fourteen straight football games and won the first state championship in UIL competition in Lubbock since Lubbock High had won state championships in the early 1950s. Dunbar had won a state championship in the old Prairie View League in 1963.

Our 1968 Estacado defense gave up only 32 points and our offense scored 552 points. That 552 points was more points than any other Lubbock team has scored in the history of the Lubbock Independent School District.

We knew we had a good football team, but we had no idea how good we were until after the season that we won the state champion-

ship. *Nineteen players received college scholarships, and ten of those players received college degrees. Our lives were forever changed!*

Coach Keeling gave us a dream! Every day for three years, he told us that we could be anything we wanted to be if we were willing to work for it.

—David Moody

The concept of "TEAM" had a huge impact on Hibbler's life.

This is a story about a group of kids that grew up together on an impoverished side of town. They had a very small window of opportunity for any success. In the United States during the 1960s, there was still a lot of racial tension. But in Lubbock, my generation seemed to have escaped most of the problems. Remind you we did stay in our neighborhood and displayed tremendous respect to our parents. The kids realized sports was one of the few ways they could enter into this window.

Along came a young white man with a great vision, believed in the word "TEAM" and the perfect coaching staff. His name is Jimmie Keeling. The coaching staff: Murrell, Garner, Gainey, Wilson, Wade, Sigman, Hampton and Nunez. Let's explore the word TEAM: "Together Each Achieve More. There is no 'I' in TEAM." Some in the black community still held reservations about Coach Keeling, but he brought to the black community a sense of pride. Coach Keeling helped open the window a little more for those kids. There are three events that shaped and molded my outlook on life.

The first event happened to one of the kids, and it left me floored, confused and not sure of the team's chances. Ted White, the twin brother of our all-state middle linebacker Fred White, never got the chance to wear a Matador uniform. He was the best athlete in school. He was a man among boys, the biggest and strongest and could run faster than almost everyone in school. The team needed him to win. The young man's mistake happened when his behavior indicated he was interested in the "I" and not the TEAM. One day at practice he was removed from the team and removed from the field. I'm sure the coaches knew the loss of this talent would hurt. I just knew losing him would be a loss, and our team would suffer from his loss.

The second event was a daily display of character and belief in "TEAM." Willie Avery may have been the smallest guy on the team, but he played one of the more important roles to our success. Willie was "The Player" on the practice squad. In preparation for each game, Willie had to be our opponent's premier running back. The defense had their work cut out for them trying to catch Willie. We were able to catch him most of the time and rough him up a little bit. Willie's desire to be a "TEAM" member and not concerned about the "I" made us all better. Willie was a giant.

The third event happened in Sweetwater. The Matadors were playing the Mustangs for the district championship, and it was a very hostile home crowd. At the half of a very close game as we entered the tunnel to our dressing room, the home crowd littered us with Coke, popcorn, hotdogs and whatever they held in their hands. The coaches assured us that we were the best "TEAM" if we continue to play together. The Matadors won the game in the second half, a game in which we could have easily quit. This was one of the biggest games of my high school career.

The lessons of these events have stayed with me all through my adult life, and I apply them often. I have been able to apply these lessons to raising my family, dealing with friends and my professional career. Thanks, Coach Keeling, for the valuable lessons. It all boiled down to TEAM: "Together Each Achieve More."

—Walter Hibbler

Following a twenty-five-year corporate career in executive roles at several Fortune 500 companies and a few information technology start-ups, Joe Rose founded Rosetta Partners, LLC, in 2003 to advise and invest in similar businesses. But, in 1968, he was the starting center for the Estacado Matadors.

Growing up in Lubbock in the 1950s and '60s, was a tale of have-a-lots, have-a-little or have-nots, with the normal blending in between these areas. Parts of town had more money and influence than other parts, of course.

Our family moved from Central Lubbock out to the new East Lubbock housing area when I was in elementary school. We moved, but we were still in lower middle class and solidly blue collar working-class neighborhoods with mortgages and a single-family car, which basically meant our fathers had regular paychecks and fairly good credit. Our neighbors were a few teachers, coaches and preachers scattered among the more typical electricians, plumbers, tile layers, paint contractors, equipment operators, truck drivers, policemen, firemen, mechanics, car salesmen and such. Most had high school educations, although the educators and ministers had college degrees. Many had served in the military during World War II. We didn't live in mixed race neighborhoods then, although we would meet some Hispanic and a few black kids in the elementary and middle schools. Since they went to our predominately white schools, we really didn't see much of the black culture through them. They acted like us mostly. I don't recall any problems between any of us then.

Fathers went to work and school sporting events, while most mothers went to PTA and kept up with teachers and their kid's progress. School had a "grade" slot for citizenship back then, and most parents took that very seriously. Teachers usually offered a comment or two on each student's report card, too. Regardless of the parent's own level of education achieved, they would expect their kids to try hard, behave and do well in school. Parents generally expected kids to be mannerly, respectful, honest and get along with others. Get in trouble or cause it, and your parents knew before you got home. Parents fed whichever kids were at their house at meal time. Kids had a lot of freedom to roam.

I was always involved with sports in school, Little League baseball and church basketball, but sports was not my life. I was not an especially gifted athlete, but I loved team sports and was pleased when my buddies picked me so I wouldn't be the last guy standing when choosing sides on the sandlot. I liked drawing and reading books, especially history and travel, and being at any activity that had lot of other kids there. Also, I actually enjoyed jobs after school and during summers.

Church was a big part of my life. Mother and I went Sunday, Wednesday and Thursday. I was in the Royal Ambassadors, a boys' youth group in our Baptist church, and always volunteered to help at Vacation Bible School and revivals.

Our family's roots are in rural small-town Arkansas, with deeper roots back to England, Ireland, Dalmatia and the Great Cherokee Nation (of the now North Georgia mountains). So, like most white people in America, our ancestors came as immigrants, except the one Native American, of course.

Most African Americans are descendants of slaves brought to America from Africa. At one point in American history, African Americans were twenty percent of the population. Today, it is closer to twelve percent. Many African American families can trace their lineage back eight to ten generations in America. My family's earliest immigrant was from England in the early 1800s, and the most recent came to America through the Port of New York in 1884. By comparisons, black populations in Europe came mostly as post WWII immigrants from Afro-Caribbean and African counties. Fewer blacks immigrated to the U.S. after WWII because of the perception of racism in America, as well as actual U.S. racial immigration quotas at the time.

We all come from somewhere, and I believe that God engineers our circumstances. The first students that attended Estacado High School in 1967 didn't choose their family's path to Lubbock and didn't have a say in the LISD Board decisions. Most didn't choose where they would attend high school. I believe that the individuals that made up the Matador football team of 1967–68 were all here for a reason: Coaches, players and staff.

I didn't consider it to be a big deal for me to go to Estacado. I saw many of the same kids I went to school, church, parties and sports with were going to be there that first year. The first student body president was one of my best friends and played piano at our church. So, even though my father decided to move us out of the area, I had committed to Coach Keeling that I would be trying out for the team in the spring of 1967. Other guys would join Estacado after moving into the area, but those would be family moves. Mine had been an individual choice. My father was against the idea, but my mother firmly supported me. Her advice to me was, "Be different if you can, life will be more interesting." So, I worked summer jobs to make the money to pay LISD out-of-district student tuition, and commute to school from our home outside of Lubbock.

By the time we got to September 5, 1967, the day the school doors first opened, the team had been through spring training, a Blue-Silver scrimmage game and two-a-days in August. I made the team. I was one of five juniors on the JV team, having spent my sophomore year at Lubbock High. Many teammates from the May '67 scrimmage had already left the school and team. Several more would leave before the 1968 season. The players that were committed were there to stay.

The racial diversity was pretty even that first year. Even so, the cultural differences between black and white students were very evident Day One. Not better or worse than the others, just different. The team had already crossed this bridge. Some students had experienced a level of racial diversity along the line, but nothing like the actual experience of a fully integrated student body. What cultural differences? Very many, actually. Shouldn't matter, of course, but at the time it was pretty interesting. Black cultural differences were evident in the ways that black students interacted with each other in the hallways, classrooms, cafeteria, pep rallies, events and even in the locker rooms. I am certain our black students had a few comments about white behavior, too. On the whole, I believe the interactions between black, white and Hispanic students was good. Many good friendships were formed in those halls and classrooms. There was some tension, some fights occurred, but that happens in all high schools between groups and among individuals. I think most people were just trying to make it work, just like the team had.

Thinking back on it, I realize that even though we were together in the same school, or on the same team, culturally we were from different neighborhoods, different churches, had different perceptions of the world, perceived different choices and opportunities available to us, ate food prepared differently, liked different music, and generally expressed ourselves more or less differently in attitude, attire and style.

To me, and I think to many of my white friends, it was very cool to become acquainted with the black culture through fellow students and appreciate the fast smiles, quick laughter, smooth body language and generally cool attitude of black students. Some of my teammates taught me the shing-a-ling [dance moves] in the shower, but I think they picked it because it was a simple step they thought even I could catch on to.

Although fewer in number, the Hispanic students were also a big part of our student body and our team. They were immediately involved in competitive athletics, student government, cheerleading and student activities. Richard Segura, Rudy Beltran, Angel Rodriguez and Enedino Samudio were stalwarts of the football program.

All this to say that, in many ways, we were from different worlds back then, and suddenly found ourselves together in an LISD attempt at integration. Across Lubbock, perceptions of the integration project were varied. A lot of misconceptions, stereotypes, parental guidance, peer influences and media reports impacted how others perceived student life at Estacado. I was friends with students from every high school in Lubbock and surrounding communities. I met with the presidents and officers of the other four high schools. Unfortunately, too many of them would ask me if our school was a safe environment, were blacks and whites getting along, or if there was constant tension in the air at school? They didn't know, and were not going to be easily convinced, that the student body was, for the most part, jelling very well. At Estacado, our differences were being accepted, and fun and friendship enjoyed across diversity lines for the most part.

I believe two things made the biggest difference between anxieties in the hallways or allowing Estacado students to actually enjoy the expe-

rience of being together. One, the educators, coaches and staff at EHS were amazing. I had never had a black teacher before. I genuinely liked each one that taught me at Estacado. I truly believe that they had been selected because they wanted to be there.

David Moody once told me that Mrs. Sheffield, one of our wonderful black educators who gave me loads of encouragement but was quick to chastise me for anything less than my best efforts in her class, was more direct with her black students. She guided them on the advantage to be realized by learning about whites in this integrated environment and explained to some that this was a different type of school experience that could provide them with a new level of appreciation for education and the advantages it offers, without the baggage of peer discouragement. I recall her quoting Ruth, Jesus' great-great-great-great grandmother: "Your present situation does not determine your future destination." These white, black, and Hispanic teachers and staff would be part of the glue that made us one student body.

The other was the immediate and continuing success of the school's winning football program. Week after week, the new school's suspect JV team playing against AAAA squads from tradition-filled schools, would win—decisively. It was fun. It was fun to anticipate, fun to prepare for, fun to support, fun pep rallies, fun to be at games and just fun to roll with. During the 1967–68 seasons, our team goals became their goals, and the student body drew strength from the victories. We all were Matadors, and winners.

As I said earlier, the summer of 1968 we would lose some more teammates to transfer. It seemed to me that parental prejudices, misconceptions or uncertainties were the cause rather than player defections.

The author has related all the best of the 1968 season highlights. All that is really left for me to do is share a few observations of some of my teammates, and I will tell you that I learned so much from being around these guys and coaches. We truly are brothers from other mothers.

—Coaches: It is amazing to me that our coaches were not that much older than the student-athletes they coached, instructed

and influenced. Nunez was an amazing trainer, and nice guy, but had the demeanor of a Marine drill instructor. Garner and Wilson were intense and led by example. Murrell was one of us. A friend for life, Jimmie Keeling was the most important educator in my life.

—Boykin and Turner: Robert Boykin always looked ready to smile. He was a bit mischievous and always fun. This man was an intense competitor. Marvin "Stroke" Turner was a genuinely loveable human being. He always looked like he had something on you, knew something you didn't and then he would break out with his laugh and big grin. He was a major hitter.

—Hibbler: Walter was a smooth and sweet fellow with a Cheshire Cat smile, but he was Mr. Intensity on the offensive and defensive line.

—Stephens: Mean Joe Green, only meaner. Freddie had the highest potential on the field.

—McLin and Benson: Street fighters in the defensive backfield. Mike and Joseph were intimidators and used arm pads like weapons. They were great defensive backs.

—Lethridge and Lester: They were quick and quicker, fast and faster. They had unmatched breakaway speed that showed up in our stats as long runs, returned kickoffs and punts for touchdowns. James could also break in front of receivers with deceptive speed. Jesse Lethridge was a bit more serious, but James Lester was great fun anytime.

—Scruggs, Morse, and Lemon: Tommy Scruggs was a great blocking tight end. He only caught a few passes in 1968, but if you read the book you know how key each was. Homer Morse was happiest on defense. He loved to hit. Of course, he

made the highlight reel in the state championship game with that interception. J. B. Lemon played both ways and also filled in as a reliable kicker whenever Miller got kicked out of the game (It happened only once).

—Wallace: Ken was the leader of the offense, the field general who could make it happen with his arm or his legs. His legs actually scored often, his arm passed some, but he usually made smooth handoffs to his great backfield.

—Hines and Hall: They were easy-going gentlemen, quick and calm but fierce in battle. Robert and William provided really great leadership by example.

—Mosley, Miller, and Judie: James Mosley was the Rock. He has this peaceful smile like a preacher, then a big grin. He was a consummate gentleman. I'm not sure if he actually wore thigh pads, or were those just his actual thighs? Larry Miller was quiet spoken. He was truly gifted as a running back and kicker, a trusted yardage maker. Frank Judie was an intense running back and consummate blocking back. He made these other guys look good behind his dependable blocks. Frank was quiet, too, but he had this knowing little smile he'd use when you amused him.

—White and Moody: Fred White was the undisputed leader of the defense, which broke every offense we played. Even Sweetwater, finally. Fred was a serious competitor. He practiced with the same intensity he played with. He didn't know many jokes himself, but he really enjoyed the good ones he heard. David Moody was also extremely competitive and a leader on defense. David was equally intense and would not allow anything less than every player's best efforts on the field. He had strong character and led by example. Both of these team leaders had a manner of discipline self-imposed

*and then enforced on team members around them. And both
of them must have been a little fragile, too, because Nunez
was always taping these guys up to hold them together before
practices and games.*

I would serve three years in the Marines after high school, including a tour of Vietnam. There I would learn that integration isn't always as easy as it seemed to go at EHS, but I would also learn that a "Team" of Marines on a hilltop could bond as brothers, too. Among veterans there is a saying, "For those who have fought for it, life has a meaning the protected will never know." As a 1967–68 Matador, I'd suggest, "For those who chose the struggle and earned victory together, our journey has a meaning others cannot fully comprehend." I would later get my college degree and find work. I was fortunate to live in three countries, work in twelve and travel to sixty-eight countries on every continent except Antarctica. Among other places, I was in apartheid South Africa, Red China, behind the Iron Curtain in [then] Czechoslovakia, Argentina during the Falklands war, and Cuba. I would see and recognize prejudice and intolerance in many places around the world. I am sure that experiences at Estacado provided me better perspective and helped me avoid misconceptions and stereotyping as I traveled to different places.

After an education corporate career, I was able to start my own advisory firm and serve on boards of public and private companies in the U.S., London, and the Philippines. I married Rolynn Mullins, and we have had three amazing sons, Johnathan, Benjamin, and Daniel. We've lived in Tampa, Atlanta and University Park [Texas]. Our sons are very familiar with the Matador story and my genuine affection for every teammate. They also know that when their dad passes, they will need a few Matador pallbearers for him.

Through it all, I have missed only two reunions and three funerals of the '68 Matadors. I genuinely love my Matador brothers.

—Joe Rose

After two years of playing football at Howard Payne, White embarked on a thirty-five-year career with Southwestern Public Service, which later became Excel. He and his wife Lucy have two daughters, Paula and Doria, and a son, Alex, along with seven grandchildren and three great-grandchildren.

In retrospect, I really don't know what would have become of me if I hadn't been able to rejoin the team after I got caught trying to skip practice during two-a-days. Coach said he would put it to the team, and they would have to vote me back on, or not. I was pretty stubborn then and prideful. I wanted to bow my back up, but I was really worried the team might not vote me back. My brother Ted was a good athlete, but he wasn't a team player, and that is why he didn't fit in with this team and coaching staff. I really wanted to be with the team, and I was glad to get that second chance. I tried hard to repay everyone with my play after that.

David Moody, Walter Hibbler, Marvin Turner, who we all called "Stroke," and many of the other guys on our team were very good friends growing up. We knew we could be a handful of trouble sometimes. We all needed the discipline the Estacado coaches expected, probably some of us more than others. It had a big impact on us.

I remember the old clunker Coach Keeling left up at the school for players that needed to use it sometimes. Everyone in the community recognized that old thing. Once we took it to the shopping center, the one with the Furr's Supermarket and the Matador Barbershop. We wanted to grab something to eat before practice. Well, it died up there and we couldn't get it started. Someone saw us and called Coach. Coach Keeling told us to leave that car and get back quick for practice.

Once, when the coaches and team went to church together at the Mackenzie Terrace Baptist Church across from the school, I remember James Mosley and Larry Miller rolling up the legs of their dress pants and commencing to do the hambone during the singing. Just seemed like it was the natural thing to do, but I think some of the teammates and coaches were a little surprised. The church members didn't seem to mind at all.

That year was a total team year. Maybe in 1967 we still had to gel a bit, but in the spring of 1968, through two-a-days and throughout the championship season, we were a team dedicated to winning together.

David Moody and I were cousins, and we got summer jobs with FarmPac, a meat processing company in Lubbock, through Roosevelt Benson, a supervisor there. Whatever you did was hard work, but the higher paying jobs were inside the plant. You started outside to get inside. It was union work, and we got union pay, too. First jobs we had started outside in the pig and cattle pens pushing them to the chutes. Then we got moved to jobs taking the animals from the chutes to the hanging room. Next, we got jobs "sticking" the animals, and then finally we got jobs on the kill floor. That was the highest pay, but it wasn't something everyone liked to do. We worked there two summers and made pretty good money.

One of my best friends was Marvin "Stroke" Turner. He was working for Lubbock Power & Light when I was working for Southwestern Public Service Company. Stroke and I liked to go to the drag races in Amarillo. We also liked to rabbit hunt. We would hunt the cotton fields behind our neighborhood. We would also head up Highway 40 toward Plainview and hunt the fields around the little town of Sundown. We liked cottontails because they were more tender than old jackrabbits. We would skin them, cut them up, flour them and skillet fry them. We would make what we called forty-weight gravy, really thick, and have a good meal. Some people tell you not to eat rabbit in a month ending in "r," but my daddy, Robert White, told us that when he was bringing rabbit home for us to eat, we didn't know or care what month it was, and neither did he. So, Stroke and I didn't care about the month, either.

When Stroke died, it was really hard. We always knew Stroke had allergies and a constant sniffle, but not really serious respiratory issues. He went in the hospital one night and died there that night. I

*got a call about midnight. I was shocked. I had just seen him that day.
Everybody took it hard. At the funeral, his family, friends, church,
and neighbors were joined by so many people from his work and just
others that came to know him. I recall seeing tears in every man's eyes
at that funeral. You know, Stroke had a way of walking that was
more like a march. His heels would hit and scoot a bit with each step,
and his shoulders seemed to dip and go back up a little with each step.
It was a proud way of walking, I thought. But it was distinctive,
too. He would stop by after work often just to visit. I would hear that
walk coming up my driveway. After he passed, I would still hear it
sometimes in the late afternoon after work coming up my driveway.*

*As for funerals among Matadors, well, I expect to have a few pall-
bearers, if any are left around. We have always attended them, whoever
was around. We always let each other know. I remember Porter Jaushlin
came by to see me a couple of weeks before he passed. I didn't really know
he was that sick. He wanted to apologize to me and ask me to forgive
him for his foolishness during practices and games at Estacado. Porter
was always out to have a good time, always smiling, kidding around.
We knew that. Sometime I would get on to him for not being serious in
practice, but he was just being Porter. He said he knew it annoyed me
and he was sorry. Next time I heard from Porter was a few weeks later.
He was in Baylor Hospital in Dallas, and Joe Rose was there with him
using his cell phone to call as many coaches and players as they could to
let Porter say his goodbyes. We all went to his funeral in Lubbock. Coach
Keeling joined several of us as a pallbearer.*

*Many us attended the funeral of our bus driver Mr. Brackett. All
of the other Matadors who have passed, their teammates have been
at their service and have been pallbearers. It is how we are. We are
family after all these years.*

—Fred White

The 1968 state champion Estacado Matadors were inducted as
a team into the Lubbock Independent School District Hall of
Honor in 2013. Then in 2016, both coach Jimmie Keeling and

quarterback Kenneth Wallace were selected individually to the LISD Hall of Honor.

Wallace, who earned a scholarship to Texas Tech and earned all-Southwest Conference honors for the Red Raiders, has enjoyed a remarkable career in education. He is currently the deputy superintendent of the Galena Park ISD near Houston.

Playing football at Estacado High School was one of the most rewarding experiences of my life. I would have never dreamed that the lessons learned from playing football would stay with me my entire life. Building leadership skills, learning responsibility, having a passion and understanding the purpose of dedication are all key attributes that I achieved from being part of the 1967, 1968, and 1969 Estacado Matador football teams.

The leadership developed when Coach Jimmie Keeling gave me the opportunity to be the starting quarterback. I loved the game of football and had some skills. However, early on in my career, I did not have very much self-confidence. Coach Keeling had a way of letting you know that you could do the job—and do it well.

He would say things like "We are going to be a good football team" and "Nobody will be able to stop us if we play the way I know that we can." He let you know his expectations, made you believe that it could be done, and that you could make it happen.

I remember during pregame meetings, Coach Keeling would have the quarterback (me) and the middle linebacker (Fred White) present the game plan to the group. I felt uncomfortable speaking in front of the team. Therefore, it was something that I did not enjoy. I was very nervous speaking in front of a group. Coach Keeling would bring me into his office and hand me a card with all the plays, formations, and special situations, and he would say this is our game plan to win the game today. I would take that card, and when it was my time to present the game plan to the team, I read the card. This process happened before each game, and it became a normal routine.

What really surprised me is that when I presented the offensive game plan, everyone listened attentively and was glued to my every word. There was no horse playing; the team took this very seriously. Little did I know that the leadership skills Coach Keeling taught me at that time would be something that I would continue to use outside of playing football (making presentations in front of groups). Today, I thank Coach Keeling for allowing me the opportunity to come out of my shell and develop self-confidence. However, the most important part was my teammates taking what I had to say seriously and making me feel as though I was becoming the leader that was expected of a quarterback.

Leading the team on the football field was never a problem. Speaking in front of the team was the most challenging. I had to be in uncomfortable situations to gain experience, learn, and develop self-confidence to build my leadership skills.

Responsibility was also something that Coach Keeling expected of us. It was our responsibility to be in school every day and on time. If you were in school, you were expected to make practice and be on time. I remember when I tried to miss a Saturday practice. Coach Keeling sent the trainer, Coach Nunez, to my home to get me. I happened to be spending the night at my cousin's house. My mother told Coach Nunez where I was. Coach Nunez found me, coaxed me out of bed, and took me to practice. Up to that point, I had never missed a practice, so when I did, Coach sent someone after me.

When we arrived at the field house, I dressed and went to the field where the team was practicing. Coach Keeling was waiting for me. He took me down to the other end of the field, away from the team. We both took a knee on the field, and Coach began to talk. He was not angry and did not raise his voice. He said, "You are very important to this football team and we are going to win a lot of football games, but you have to be here for us to do that." He points to the team and said, "All of those guys are depending on you, and I know you don't want to let them down." He looked at me and said, "Let's go to work."

This was a sobering moment for me to know that I was actually needed and that the team was counting on me. Everyone wants to feel needed and feel important, and this was the feeling that Coach Keeling left me with that day. A person who feels appreciated will always do more than what is expected. When you are fifteen or sixteen years old, you don't think much about feelings, but they are important. Instead of Coach yelling at me and making me run lots of wind sprints, he just spoke to me like a person who cared. That is a sign of a good leader. Although, after practice that day, I did have to run for the time missed. While I was running, many of my teammates stayed out to watch. By the way, I took it like a man.

One thing about our football team is that we were passionate about the game. We loved playing football. The reason we were so passionate about football was because of the immediate feedback that we received. You did not have to have someone telling you how well you were playing. During a football game, you could look at the scoreboard and see how you were playing as a team. If there were not many points on the board during the first quarter, the team would quickly make those corrections. If my memory serves me right, I don't think there were many times that our opponents had more than seven points on the scoreboard.

Our team continued to improve as the season progressed. The team became known as scoreboard watchers, which was our way of determining whether we were being successful or not. The immediate feedback from the game kept us passionate and dedicated to playing the game. We could not wait to return to school and/or practice the following Monday. We loved being in school so much because practice was fun and we could not wait to do it all over again. In fact, we practiced fourteen weeks in a row—all the way to the state championship game!

Looking back at the 1968 state championship, it was one of the biggest accomplishments in my life. Not the biggest, but one of the biggest, and I look forward to and expect that same type of success in everything that I have been involved in. The team developed strong work ethic during the 1968 season. Still, to this day, I dedicate myself to the same work ethic in all of my endeavors. I learned that nothing worthwhile comes easy. You have to dedicate yourself and work hard for it.

The success, dedication, hard work and responsibility gained from being part of this Matador team guided me on a path that has led me to where I am today.

Full scholarship to Texas Tech University
Sun Bowl 1972, Gator Bowl 1973
All-Southwest Conference honors 1973
Player in the 1974 College All-American Game
Graduation Texas Tech 1974
Master's degree Texas Tech 1979
Head football coach 1980–87
Football coach of the year 1981, 1982, and 1987
Principal 1989–2011 (Lubbock Estacado and Houston
*   Galena Park North Shore)*
Principal of the Year 2005–06 Galena Park ISD
Region IV Principal of the Year 2006–07
Principal of the Year 2009–10 Galena Park ISD
Assistant Superintendent Galena Park ISD
Associate Superintendent Galena Park ISD
Deputy Superintendent Galena Park ISD 2014-present

—Kenneth Wallace

Unlike most of the other players who grew up in east Lubbock, Scruggs grew up in Tulia.

When I showed up at Estacado in the fall of 1967, I knew Coach Keeling, Coach Garner, and a girl named Linda Newburn. The coaches had coached me at Tulia before coming to Estacado, and I had met Linda in the summer of 1966, between my ninth and tenth grade. After arriving at Estacado, Linda and I became friends.

It was during the first week at Estacado that I found out that I was going to have to play on the JV team because of the transfer eligibility rule. I had played on the varsity team at Tulia before coming to Estacado. It was while I was sitting in English class, I thought on this and decided to go to the office and check myself out of Estacado and beat a path back to Tulia. I got up, left the room and headed to the office. I hadn't gone far before I met my dad and the principal Mr. Rice, coming down the hall. My dad told me that the family had found a house to rent and that he now had a job in Lubbock. I smiled and told them how glad I was and then returned to my English class.

That first year had its challenges. It seemed like we scrimmaged the varsity nearly every day. I broke my arm in the last game of my first year at Estacado. I was glad the season was over and started to look forward to what was ahead. After my arm healed, I began working out with the varsity during the off season.

I wasn't sure how to take the guys. One minute they were talking trash, acting like a bunch of clowns, and the next minute they were as serious as they could be. They could hit you hard, extremely hard. Sometimes they were hiding from Coach and other times they were dazzling him with what they could do. I tried to take it all in stride. If I was going to make the team, it was going to take all I had plus a good bit of luck. They were comfortable in their element. I was out of mine.

That summer I got a job working for the City Park Department. By this time, Linda and I had become good friends and we saw each other about every day. Many days she would bring me lunch and we could find some shade and sit and talk.

Soon summer was coming to a close, my job was coming to an end, and two-a-days were starting. Football season was underway. Nobody had a clue what was in store for us. How the coaches kept that bunch of guys going in the same direction is a mystery to me. Shortly after school started, I got a job working at the neighborhood grocery store. Joe Rose was already working there, and a couple of others were as well. It was a good place for us guys to work. Fred White and David

Moody worked at FarmPac on the kill floor. We all were doing what we needed to do to stay in the game.

It was about the second week of school that I found out my family was moving to Pampa. If I was going to play ball, I needed to stay in Lubbock. I got a room in a rooming house in downtown Lubbock for $30 a month, bills paid. It was me and three old men that lived there. It wasn't much, but good enough.

The weeks rolled by and we were winning our games. I was out late one night after a Friday night game. I was broke and out of gas. I made a bad decision. I had a gas can in the trunk of my car. I cut off a three-foot piece of water hose, jumped a fence in a construction area and was about to get me a little gas when I found myself in the beam of a police car's spotlight. The officer hauled me into the city jail and put me in the drunk tank with the most hideous men I had ever seen. You got a dried-up egg sandwich for breakfast and a dried-up bologna sandwich for supper and all the water you could drink. No pillow, no blanket and no mattress. I was there the rest of that night, Saturday and Sunday. I was given one phone call. I did not call my dad. That would have been worse than being in jail. I called Linda.

Monday morning Coach Keeling asked Linda where I was and she told him I was in jail. Later that afternoon, the jailer came to my cell and told me that my principal and coach had arranged for my release. I was back at school in time for the afternoon workout. I learned a hard lesson. As far as I know, nobody ever knew I had gotten into trouble, and for that I was thankful.

The weeks that followed were filled with hard work and victories. A bunch of guys from the east side were making history. We all had a story to tell. We all were plain old everyday east side boys that got caught up in a West Texas football storm that hurled us down the road of life and prepared us for much of what life has dealt us.

Hats off to the coaching staff of that team. Looking back, I find it remarkable how we came together and even to this day, rest in the friendships we find in one another. I am thankful that I stuck around.

Could it be that God's hand was working that bunch of east side boys?

By the way, I married that girl I met that summer of 1966, and Linda and I celebrated our forty-seventh wedding anniversary on June 7, 2016. She is still my best friend.

—Tommy Scruggs

Of course, it was Coach Keeling who put the pieces together for Estacado's record-setting season.

This was the Best of Times for me as a coach. I had the privilege of coaching football for fifty-six years. I coached high school football for thirty-five years and college football for twenty-one years. All were great for me, but none better than the days at Estacado High School. I was hired as the head football coach at Estacado High School in Lubbock at the age of thirty-one. At this young age, I had been a high school assistant for four years and a head coach for eight years.

In my eyes, the Estacado job was a great opportunity for me personally. Being in a brand new high school and starting a program from scratch was very appealing to me.

I absolutely know now that God placed me at this particular place at this specific time in history. I also believe God placed each of the individual players at this place at this time. Honestly, I don't believe I ever saw this so much as a new integrated school as I thought about it as a fantastic opportunity.

We began immediately to conduct an intense off-season program with this group of young athletes, assembling daily at Alderson Junior High. These were mostly Alderson students, but also some from Struggs Junior High and a small number from Dunbar and Lubbock High. As a coaching staff, we coached these young men very hard, and they responded in a positive manner. They stepped up and met every challenge. They were remarkable listeners and wanted to achieve, not only in football but academically and in their personal lives.

It was obvious immediately that we had some very special young people and very talented athletes. Speed was a significant factor with this group.

One of the most important factors from my standpoint was that this group was not only talented, but had a great desire to work hard and excel at being players. They had a love for the game of football and played it with a passion. They thrived on winning!

A huge factor was the willingness of many great athletes who had been backs and were willing to become players at other positions. They became offensive and defensive linemen, linebackers, and secondary players—and they excelled at those positions. They were truly unselfish.

Another big factor was that we assembled a superior coaching staff that was perfect for this time and place, and they wanted to be there. Our varsity coaches were Delbert Wilson, Gene Murrell, Wayne Garner, and Hollis Gainey. They also loved and cared about these players, and they excelled at coaching and motivating these great young people. E. G. Nunez was our athletic trainer and played a significant role in building a successful program.

Not only was our football staff outstanding, but our administration and staff and the teaching staff were hand-picked and were truly outstanding.

The Lubbock ISD athletic director was Pete Ragus, and he developed a situation for us at Estacado that was very conducive to excellence in football. Pete Ragus influenced my life immensely.

We were expected to play in AAAA football and were allowed spring football that first spring. At that time, AAAA was the top UIL division. When the numbers came in later that fall, it was determined we would be in AAA. The first season in 1967, we won nine games and lost one playing AAAA junior varsity teams.

We entered the fall of 1968 with high expectations for this outstanding group. The book itself tells about how all of this occurred. The great thing is that this team went 14–0 and won the state championship, putting up great offensive, defensive, and kicking team stats.

It was a magical season, and as you read the book, hopefully you enjoyed this amazing team and its success. This team and this group of young men found a way to develop an unusually great team unity. These players and coaches saw no color except Matador blue!

These players worked extremely hard to become an outstanding team. Our team discipline was outstanding, and the strong leadership by the players themselves was largely responsible for this. Another major reason for our success at Estacado was having great parent support.

From my standpoint, this group achieved true greatness as a team. Even more importantly, they developed into outstanding young men. What they achieved as a team was exceptional. What they have achieved after that time is even more rewarding. They truly have become incredible men who make a difference in our world.

It would be wonderful if every coach that truly loves and cares about young men could have the experience that I had at Lubbock Estacado High School. Even more importantly, I believe it would be a treat if every high school football player—and even every student for that matter—could experience what those young men got to experience. The way they learned to trust, believe in, depend on, and love each other was truly phenomenal. The world would be a better place if all young people could have the experience this group had and respond as they did.

Even today, almost fifty years later, this group of players and their coaches have strong bonds and relationships and ties to each other and stay in close contact. These young men made the most of the talents God gave them.

About the 1968 Matadors, it is easy to say "Once a Matador, always a Matador!" What a joy and pleasure to have had the honor coaching these special men!

"WE ARE THE MATADORS—THE MIGHTY, MIGHTY MATADORS!"

—Jimmie Keeling

Appendix

Lubbock Estacado Matador Football Season Summary, 1968

Estacado, Points Scored	Opponent, Points Scored
14	Brownfield, 0
51	Littlefield, 0
33	Lamesa, 0
69	Levelland, 0
28	Lubbock Dunbar, 0
73	San Angelo Lake View, 6
60	Slaton, 6
54	Snyder, 0
42	Colorado City, 0
7	Sweetwater, 0
49	Brownwood, 8
28	Kermit, 12
30	Henderson, 0
14	Refugio, 0
Totals **552**	**32**

Football Team Roster, 1968

Number	Name	Position	Weight	Class
11	Jesse Bozeman	QB	155	Junior
12	Kenneth Wallace	QB	152	Junior
14	Daniel Johnson	QB	156	Sophomore
20	Jesse Lethridge	TB	137	Sophomore
21	Marvin Turner	TB	156	Junior
24	Mike McLin	E	160	Senior
31	Frank Judie	FB	182	Junior
32	James Mosley	FB	201	Junior
34	Porter Jaushlin	FB	216	Sophomore
40	James Lester	WB	146	Senior
41	Joe Benson	TB	148	Junior
42	Avance Green	WB	146	Senior
44	Larry Miller	TB	173	Junior
50	Joe Rose	C	170	Senior
52	Mike Eller	C	171	Senior
54	Richard Segura	C	162	Junior
60	Bobby Lester	G	165	Junior
61	Kenny Williams	T	177	Sophomore
62	Robert Boykin	G	162	Junior
63	Ruben Romero	G	145	Senior
64	Walter Hibbler	G	178	Junior
65	Gene Null	G	175	Sophomore
66	Enedino Samudio	G	156	Junior
67	J.B. Lemon	G	170	Junior
70	Floyd Harris	T	170	Sophomore
71	Rudy Beltran	T	174	Senior

72	Robert Hines	T	175	Senior
73	Dean Null	T	178	Sophomore
74	William Hall	T	171	Junior
75	Homer Morse	T	175	Senior
77	Angel Rodriquez	T	198	Sophomore
78	David Hightower	T	180	Junior
80	David Moody	E	168	Junior
81	Ronnie Hill	E	140	Senior
83	Fred White	T	180	Senior
84	Freddie Stephens	E	192	Junior
85	Tyson Haynes	E	149	Sophomore
87	Tommy Scruggs	E	173	Senior

Coaches: Jimmie Keeling, head coach; Delbert Wilson, Wayne Garner, Gene Murrell, Hollis Gainey, R. A. Wade
Athletic Trainer and Coach: E. G. Nunez
Managers: Larry Blanchard, Steve Gentry, Melvin Mitchell
Student Trainers: Garry Garrett, Scott Harmon, Billy McGinnis

In Memoriam (as of March 2017)

#21, Marvin "Stroke" Turner
#34, Porter Jaushlin
#42, Avance Green
#60, Bobby Lester
#62, Robert Boykin
#70, Floyd Harris
#74, William Hall
#78, David Hightower
#82, Buddy King
#84, Freddie Stephens
Coach Gene Murrell
Coach Hollis Gainey
Athletic Trainer and Coach E. G. Nunez

Index

About the Author

Al Pickett, who was inducted into the Big Country Athletic Hall of Fame in Abilene, Texas, in 2016, has spent more than forty years covering high school and college sports.

Mighty, Mighty Matadors is Pickett's fifth book. He has also coauthored *Wishbone Wisdom: Emory Bellard, Texas Football Visionary*, with the former Texas A&M head football coach who invented the wishbone offense; *Team of the Century*, chronicling the seven years that Chuck Moser spent as the head football coach at Abilene High; *The Greatest Texas Sports Stories You've Never Heard*; and *Brother's Keeper: The Story of the 2009 Abilene High State Championship*, coauthored with Abilene minister Chad Mitchell, chaplain of the Abilene High football team. A cinematic treatment of *Brother's Keeper* is under development for 2017.

Pickett, who spent fifteen years at sports editor of the *Abilene Reporter-News*, is the host of "Let's Talk Sports," a call-in radio sports talk show in Abilene, and is the play-by-play voice for Abilene High, Abilene Cooper, and Hardin-Simmons University athletics on the radio.

He is also a freelance writer and owns his own business, Pickett Publications and Sales, which publishes the *West Central Texas Oil Activity Index*, a daily and weekly reporting service for oil-related businesses.

Pickett is a regular contributor to *Dave Campbell's Texas Football*, *Red Raider Sports*, *Permian Basin Oil and Gas*, *Well Servicing*, and *American Oil and Gas Reporter*. He received the Outstanding

Media Service Award from the American Southwest Conference in 2004 and is a past president of the Texas Associated Press Sports Editors.

Pickett is a native of Council Grove, Kansas, and a graduate of Kansas State University, with a degree in journalism and mass communications. He and his wife Carole have two sons and four grandchildren.